Harry's War

G Southall-Owen

Copyright © 2018 Geoffrey Southall-Owen

All rights reserved. This publication may not be reproduced, stored in a retrieval system or transmitted in any form or by any means, electronic, mechanical, photocopying, recording or otherwise, without permission in writing from the author.

ISBN-13: 978-1718650015

ISBN-10: 1718650019

FOR MY GRANDFATHER

This book is based on the memoirs of my grandfather, Harry Southall-Owen. He was quite a literary man, he wrote poetry and short stories which were published in local papers. He wrote a detailed account of his experiences before and during the Second World War. He also wrote several pieces on the history of his hometown, Bilston, much of this history was an account of daily life living in the heart of the Black Country in the 60's era. He was well liked and respected by many in the community, he was so knowledgeable about his hometown, quite a few of the locals gave him the nickname 'Mr Bilston.' He was invited to give talks about local history at schools and colleges throughout the area. Harry passed away in January 2000, just a few days before his 92nd birthday. This book gives you an insight in to the life of an ordinary man, who by his courage and determination and his immeasurable sense of adventure lived the most extraordinary life.

CONTENTS

ACKNOWLEDGEMENTS

PREFACE

	PICTURES OF HARRY	I
	PROLOGUE	IV
I	MY LIFE UP TO THE AGE OF TEN	1
II	INDUSTRIAL SCHOOL	15
III	THE BIRCH	18
IV	LEAVING SCHOOL	32
V	GENTLEMAN TRAMP	34
VI	JOINING THE ARMY	40
VII	ON THE RUN	43
VIII	GLASSHOUSE	45
IX	MALTA	48
X	PALESTINE	54
XI	FRENCH FOREIGN LEGION	59
XII	UNEMPLOYMENT SECRETARY	73
XIII	BATTLES WITH THE MOSLEYITES	75
XIV	RE-JOINING THE ARMY	82
XV	PROMOTION	86

XVI	CHANGING MY NAME	91
XVII	EVACUATION OF SAINT MALO	94
XVIII	GLIDER PILOT REGIMENT	101
XIX	RETURN TO UNIT	108
XX	REVERSION OF RANK	113
XXI	INVASION OF NORTH AFRICA	115
XXII	INVASION OF ITALY	122
XXIII	GIBRALTAR	125
XXIV	HOME AND DE-MOBBED	130
XXV	BARROW FILLER	132
XXVI	STREET VENDOR	137
XXVII	SHOP AND MOBILE COACH	143
XXVIII	MANAGER	150
XXIX	BANKRUPT	154
XXX	HOUSE HUNTING	158
XXXI	GETTING A JOB	160

It's your road, and yours alone

Others may walk it with you

But no one can walk it for you

RUMI

ACKNOWLEDGMENTS

The first acknowledgment must be to my grandfather, Harry Southall-Owen and whom this book is about. I grew up listening to countless stories of years gone by and my grandfather's time serving in the military and was no doubt one of the contributing factors of why I ended up joining the military. It's not until years have passed that you appreciate the hardships endured by the older generations. He lived through the Great War, the Great Depression, and then served in the Second World War, struggling with post war rationing while trying to bring up a large family. He documented everything and had a passion for writing. All this made the book possible, but this was no easy task collating all the information. I would like to thank the Black Country Bugle for allowing me to use information on the Batman's Hill boiler explosion which involved my great, great grandfather and the Forces War Records who provided me with information on different locations of the army regiments before and during the Second World War. I would like to thank the late Dr Chris Upton reader in Public History at Newman University Birmingham, with the article on my grandfather and Frank Gray MP written in the Birmingham Post Dec 2013.

This book initially was for the family and friends to look back on over the years but I feel this story should be available to anyone who may have an interest in the history of the local area. I would like to thank Lisa Watkins for proof reading the book for me.

I would like to thank my Dad, Ron for keeping photographs, letters and other vital information. My uncle Harry for telling me the stories from the shop. Finally, I would like to thank all my aunties, and uncles and my cousins. Throughout my childhood especially on Saturday afternoons we would listen to stories retold by about my grandfather and grandmother of their earlier lives.

ABOUT THE AUTHOR

Geoff Southall-Owen is the grandson of Harry. He served over two decades as a Royal Marine Commando and is now retired from the military. Inspired by childhood stories told by his grandfather and in possession of his grandfather's memoirs he thought it would be a fitting tribute to a great, yet humble man to write this book about his grandfather's remarkable life. The historical facts of the Second World War are well documented, this is a personal account of how life was at the time. This is a story of Harry's War.

Preface

One of the earliest memories of my grandfather was when he got me a paper round. He knew the shop keepers in the area, notably a post office in Ettingshall village. It was owned by three sisters. He got me the job which covered the street where he lived, so he could have his paper delivered nice and early in the morning. He would wake me up at six o'clock every morning, my Mum and Dad and I lived with my Nan and Grandad. He would time me to see how long it would take me, and then tell me to do it quicker the next day. First thing he would say was, "WHAT TOOK YA." He would help me on most mornings in all weathers, realising now he must have been in his seventies. "Fit as a fiddle," he would say. Every morning before we left he would listen to Radio 4 Shipping Forecast an example would be, 'Tyne, Humber, Northeast 3 or 4. Occasional rain, moderate or poor.' We would listen to this while I had my cereal, I would say, "Grandad why are we listening to this? we are miles away from the coast," the simple reply would be "Sssh." I thought it was some secret code he was listening to waiting for some military orders. Each day after school, I would do my evening paper round, Grandad would be standing outside the house looking at his watch waiting for the evenings Express & Star newspaper. It must have been around this time that told him I was interested in joining the Royal Marines.

He would gather the kids in the street and make us race one another notably against Michael James who could run like the wind, no one could beat him, or watch us wrestle his brother Billy James, again we couldn't beat him either but playing on the street kept us kids fit. My grandmother would send my grandfather and me to the shops, we would be gone for hours, every few yards he would stop and talk to the neighbours something that doesn't happen now.

Later in his life, Harry and I would sit for hours, discussing my military career and swopping war stories, although Harry's war experiences were very different to mine. He kept Canaries and he would be in the shed for hours maybe just reflecting on the life he had led over the years. He was just a matter of fact sort of man. Looking back on his life it was more than the ordinary, it was very extraordinary.

Sergeant H Southall-Owen, World War 2
Picture taken in 1942 The Glider Pilot Regiment

Harry and Lilian in the mobile shop early 1950's

Harry was fond of local history (1986)

Prologue

It was a warm summer's evening, and I was drifting off to sleep thinking of my young family back home, and wondering if my wife had received my letters.

"Sergeant Owen, Sarge, the commanding officer and Major Proctor want to speak to you!" it was our company clerk, Private Oliver.

"Now," he said.

He was normally a reserved sort of chap his change of demeanour told me I was needed for, so something was important.

It was the 15th June 1940. My battalion were using the football ground in Rennes, France, as a camping ground, we occupied the pitch, the only part of France that we could say was ours. We were retreating, making our way back to the French coast. France was beginning to fall to the Germans, Paris was now under Nazis control, every major city west of Paris including Rennes would be one of the next to be occupied by the Nazis. We were waiting for orders to move to the port of Saint Malo, *'Jerry'*, were moving in on us fast. We were the last of the British troops on French soil.

We all know about the Dunkirk evacuation there's been many a book, film or documentary about it. The military codename for it was Operation Dynamo, it occurred between the 26th May and the 4th June 1940, when civilian boats came to the rescue and saved over three hundred thousand troops from the shores of France. It's now two weeks later and my battalion are still in France. We were stationed about three hundred miles to the west and had been told that we were being evacuated from the port of Saint Malo, France, in one days' time, under the code name Operation Ariel. I picked up my Mk 4 .303 Lee-Enfield rifle, then grabbing my Brodie tin helmet headed over to the company commander and my battalions commanding officer, I was the senior sergeant in my battalion at the age of 32. On the way over in my mind I was confused about what could be wrong. Were we being delayed again? Are we moving to the port? Had the sentries I posted out earlier, or the wandering patrol spotted any enemy?

"Sergeant Owen," the commanding officer greeted me.

"Intelligence has been passed on to us, that a military train loaded with *'Jerry'*, are moving from the east and heading for Rennes. I want you to select five other men including a corporal. Move by foot ten miles east of Rennes, find some cover and blow the rail track. This will slow down *'Jerry'*, giving our chaps more time to embark on the boats. It's a delaying tactic! "Any questions?" I looked at him blankly.

"No? Well get a move on, tally ho! There's a war on." As I walked back I chose the five names in my mind. I had been working with them for months and I knew the capabilities of every one of my troops. I gathered the company around me. I raised my voice,

"Close in everyone. I need five volunteers for a

patrol this evening." Pop Dyson's hand went up straight away.

"Can't take you, Pop, you're sixty-seven, you old git,"

"No, I'm not," he replied. Everyone laughed.

"I need to pick five men, listen in."

"Charlie, George, Jack, Bill, and Bobby," who was a former Royal Engineer, now one of my corporals. To me the fittest and smartest guys in the company. I had a keen eye for men I could trust with my life but also men who could think on their feet. I told them the plan, we didn't have much time. I could see the excitement in their faces and the disapproval in the faces of the men I didn't select. I told them to get some more ammunition, we filled our water canteens, and checked our rifles. Bobby would be laying the two sticky bombs under the track it was primarily used for sticking on the side of a tank as an anti-tank mine I thought it would cut through the track or at least derail a train. Bobby decided to take two sticky bombs, just in case one didn't work. They didn't work well sticking to anything muddy or wet so if the tracks are covered in dirt we could tie them to it using a bit of wire. We have time on our side, it's not like we have to stick them to the side of a moving tank. It had two pins, the first of which would arm the mechanism, and the second would ignite the nitro-glycerine. Once the wire was released the lever would open, which would activate a five second fuse. Using the wire, we would trail it back over the blind side of the embankment. The bomb was still being trialled by the battalion it was a new bit of equipment, it was rushed into service like most of the equipment we had but we would take it. It was now 21.00 hours, it was summertime and it was beginning to get dark, we shall leave in one hour.

As we moved off I told the men to have a decent gap between each man as we patrol across country, and to stay alert as we were heading back into enemy held territory. Let me know if you hear or see anything suspicious. We needed to avoid any civilians, they couldn't be trusted, and to keep off the roads *Jerry'* could be lurking anywhere.

When we left the stadium, a Saturday evening at around 22.00, a clear night, you could see the stars shining brightly, the town was eerily quiet, the odd dog barking in the distance. I knew the area from our previous foot patrols I knew where to find the rail line. We crossed the road into a farmer's field, and it was so quiet you could have heard a pin drop. I set my compass to east, making sure I kept the rail track to my left. Bobby, the corporal, was my tail end man, and I could trust him with my life. I knew that further on along the field was the start of a horse or sheep trail, which was covered by bushes, that concealed us from the open ground. It ran adjacent to the rail track. Moving along the field I noticed a dark silhouette about forty yards in front of me. My heart began to pound in my chest, but as I crept closer I could make out the outline better, it was a cow chewing on some grass. I took a deep breath. If *'Jerry'* found us now there is no rescue, no troops to come looking for us. We were on our own. Maybe being shot as saboteurs or dragged off to Colditz ran through my mind. At the corner of the field I could see the farmers gate, we climbed over and onto the other side of the trail. The trail crossed the tracks half a mile on, this confused me a little I was going to keep the track to my left. I stopped to check my map, well it was a sketch that I drew from the company commander's map. We mere mortals hardly ever saw a map, not until later in the war. I checked the distance that we had covered. I reckoned the patrol was between the La Vilaine river, to the left and the rail track to my right. That was fine for navigation but for an escape we would be boxed in by the river. Once I was reassured it was safe we proceeded. Moving much quicker, we eventually came to a village called Cesson-Sévigné, with the river running through it. I could just make out some lights in the distance. I decided we should blow the track five hundred yards east of the next village Noyal-sur-Vilaine. We were still channelled between the river to the north and the rail track to the south, and we were moving directly east. The ground was open flat country-side, not much cover for a six-man patrol. We decided to move down towards the river to benefit from better camouflage against the treeline. I could hear the water gushing as we got closer. Between the odd cloud, an almost full moon beamed down onto the countryside helping our navigation. I could just make out the silhouette of the church tower, it is the village of Noyal-sur-Vilaine. It was 02.00hrs and I calculated we had walked for about 9.6 miles. If we breach the tracks now, I thought, that leaves us four hours to return to the stadium by first light at 06.00hrs.

Once in position we waited a couple of minutes to make sure no one had seen or followed us, and then we made our way from the river and headed directly to the rail line. At the embankment I signalled to Bobby to fix the bombs to the track, one on the underneath and the other on top to cut the steel in half. Charlie and George were acting as lookouts as, Bill and Jack started to unravel the wire from the track back over the embankment, this would provide us with some cover from the explosion. Once Bobby had removed the stones from underneath the track he placed the sticky bomb under the track meaning the blast would go upwards. If it didn't cut the track it would certainly lift it up from the railway sleepers. We reckoned it would be enough for a derailment. Bobby placed the wire around the triggers and removed the first pin, then stuck the bombs to the rail. We retreated over the embankment and waited. Bobby had said while his hand was on the track he could feel vibrations. George and Charlie came back and they thought they had heard the noise of a train. I was the old sergeant, I couldn't hear anything only the noise of the water cascading along the river. In my mind I tried to block out the noise and listen for something else when Charlie shouted out.

"There's a train coming."
"Pull the wire," I yelled.

There was a five second pause which seemed to last forever then an almighty flash followed by a bang. The earth shuddered. Stones and dust rained down on us, with bits of debris pinging off our tin helmets. My hearing was now reduced to a single high-pitched tone. I gave the command to move we got up and began to run west heading for Rennes. Adrenalin pumped through my body, my heart trying to jump through my chest. We must have ran for a mile with the rest of the patrol gradually overtaking me. As I was the older one, I started to struggle for breath. "Over here," I gasped. The lads gathered in, grabbed some water, and then we heard what I can only describe as the sound of thunder with the ground vibrating, which lasted for a few seconds. Had the train derailed? I felt a sudden surge of guilt running through my mind.

"What if French civvies are on board?" I called out. "Not at this time of the morning there's not," Jack shouted back. "It must be full of bloody Germans."

How many Nazis were injured or killed? It played on my mind throughout the rest of the war, until near the end when British troops found the first of many concentration camps. Did I feel guilty then? "Did I hell!"

It was now 0430hrs, Sunday 16th June 1940, we had a ship to catch onward to Blighty…and so begins Harry's story.

Chapter I

MY LIFE UP TO THE AGE OF TEN

Before the First World War began in 1914, I used to run away from home and sleep out at night. For this, I would appear before the local Juvenile Magistrates. Between these escapades, I led an ordinary life, which at that time was rather hard.

I start to relate my adventure from Tuesday 28th January 1908, the date of my birth to the end of the Great War in 1918, giving you an insight to the kind of life and conditions that the poor class lived in.

My birth was rather difficult, my mother told me, touch and go whether I make it or not, which in those days, in the slums of the Black Country, infant mortality was common amongst us poor folk. I was one of a large family, there was my father, my mother, three brothers and four sisters. My mother was married to Joseph Owen but by now they were separated and she had found companionship with a lodger at the house by the name of Adam Southall, a good-looking chap who served in the Boer War. On my birth certificate my surname is Owen, my middle name Southall, and my first name Henry. So, reading from that, my mother still had her married name of Owen, Southall being the lodger, and Henry the name they gave me. I never questioned it. The time to put a hyphen in my name making it double barrelled, I describe later in this book. It was never spoken about in those days, everything was all kept very quiet. It still confuses the family today. Don't think I am well to do for having a double-barrelled name, far from it, I'm proud to know where I came from, the working-class.

We lived up an entry in a house alongside seven more houses. Each house comprised of a kitchen, pantry, and two bedrooms, father and mother in one bedroom, brothers and sisters in the other one with sheets or blankets dividing them. The lighting in these rooms were candles with an oil lamp in the kitchen. You would be regarded as posh to have gas in those days. For sanitation, there would be one shared lavatory per four families, which was approximately thirty people. This would be a piece of wood over a bin, like a dustbin. Sometimes you would have to wait your turn to use the lavatory and if one of the adults came they would jump in front of you and you couldn't say anything otherwise came a clip around the ear. Each communal backyard had what we called '*ash pits*,' which were what ash, potato peelings and other refuse was emptied into. We would also put ash in the lavatory, not only to mask the raw sewage smell but also to cut down on flies in the summer months. Workmen employed by the Urban District Council *UDC,* emptied the toilets once a week, and ours were emptied on a Friday evening. Two men would carry the bin down the entry at about midnight, empty the contents into what we called an *'iron bogey'* and it was pulled away by a horse.

There was no water system to these closets. Bathing of the children in our house fell on a Saturday night. This was an occasion! Our bathtub was the top of a beer barrel that had been sawn off about twelve inches from the top. It was three quarter filled with water and placed on the hearthrug in front of the coal fire, and our mother used to bath us in turns. The other part of the tub was used to do the washing in, in the room that we called the *'Bruce',* brew house.

My father worked at Alfred Hickman's later called Stewart & Lloyds. His wage was about eighteen shillings for horse driving. Public houses were open from 6am till 11pm. Many times, my mother sent me to see if my father was in the boozer, instead of going to work. One of my favourite recollections is riding up Oxford Street in Bilston on the back of a tram, holding onto the lamp, with the conductor hitting away at me with his time sheet board to make me get off.

Other events stand out more distinctly, sometimes we would pass the ironworks where my grandfather was killed in an explosion, no such thing as 'Health & Safety' in those days.

The story my father told me was that James Warren, a family man aged forty-one, left his home in Wesley Street, Bradley, Bilston to pay a visit to Tupper and Companies Ironworks, at Batman's Hill, Bilston. He should have been with his wife at the annual tea party at Saint Martin's Church, but as the mill manager at the works, he felt it his duty, to check on how the new boiler was working. In truth, it was anything but new, the company had purchased it from another firm, the week before.

It was a dark, cold, winters night on Tuesday 20th January 1903, as he stood beside the boiler, while a frantic Henry Southall, my grandfather the engine driver, vainly tried to plug a leak with his cold hands on the main joint of the boiler. It was the last thing he and the driver saw, as the overloaded boiler exploded, it killed them both instantly. The blast destroyed the building which housed the boiler, badly damaged the rest of the works, and flung huge chunks of metal more than a hundred yards. The residents of both Rose Street, and Wesley Street, who couldn't have failed to realise what had happened, rushed to the factory gates in such numbers that a doctor, alerted by a patient, had difficulty reaching the scene. Thirteen other men were quickly rushed off to Wolverhampton General Hospital, where sadly later that night, two more died from their injuries. James Warrens wife, was on the way to the works, from Slater Street, when she heard from another woman, that men had died, and that the works manager was one of them. The death toll would have been a lot higher, if the number two mill had been in use as well. There were two inquests, the first at The Victoria Inn, in Wesley Street, Bradley, and the second at Wolverhampton Town Hall. The company's managing director, E.C. Lewis, the works' chief engineer, James Higgs, and the man who passed the boiler fit to use, Francis Hill, faced a barrage of questions from the government inspectors. Hill was severely criticised, for his lax approach to safety, considering that he had failed to spot the boiler tubes were clogged with dirt. They could not however, pin a charge on any of the management team, and the result was predictable, accidental death.

All the dead men had families, and the widows were left in dire need following the tragedy. My father helped my grandmother, Mary Southall, financially who had another four children to feed. That's probably why we were so poor. If it hadn't been for the community's generosity, the other families would have starved. The dead men were named as:

Henry Southall, aged 39, my grandfather the Engine Driver, Stoke Street, Daisy Bank, Bilston.

James Warren, aged 41, Mill Manager, Wesley Street, Bradley, Bilston.

Edward Holloway, aged 36, Roller, Wellington Road, Bilston.

Richard Cooper, aged 46, Furnaceman, Hall Green Street, Bradley, Bilston.

My hometown of Bilston is situated two miles southeast of Wolverhampton, in the heart of the Black Country playing its part in the Industrial Revolution. It was a manufacturing powerhouse, the furnaces lit up the skies at night. It was rumoured that Queen Victoria travelling through on the train peered through the curtains and through sheer disgust seeing the thick black smoke she called it the Black Country. Others reckon it is the abundance of coal which ran through the area. Mine shafts scattered the area, everywhere, even today the odd house can suffer from subsidence due to the foundations being built on old mineshafts.

Whatever the reason Bilston and its history certainly helped build an empire. Bilston was its own independent town until 1966 then it became under the control of Wolverhampton. It was formerly in the county of South Staffordshire but now in the county of the West Midlands. The Birmingham Canal runs through the town and so did two rail lines which closed in 1972 and one being replaced by a tramline. At the turn of the 19th Century Bilston's economy was based on farming. In the early 1900's the town transformed into an industrial heartland with numerous factories and coal mines. The industrialist John Wilkinson built a blast furnace here in 1748. In my later life I officiated the opening of the 'The John Wilkinson School.' I also wrote a manuscript about him.

One of my favourite sleeping out places was at the Steel Works Hickman's, in Bilston. My mother used to report me missing to the police, the search would begin to find me. Once, when I knew that my mother and elder brothers were looking out for me, I asked an old watchman to hide me in a bag of coal. I was of the wandering type and it was quite usual for the police to bring me home from different towns on the crossbars of their cycles. This would be at about midnight or the early hours of the morning and they would ask my mother if she had counted her *'chickens'*. My two favourite Bilston policemen were Sergeant George Cartwright and Detective Daniels, who were very good to me.

I remember in 1914. I was seven. I saw a poster around Bilston Town that I had never seen before. It was Lord Kitchener, the Secretary of State for war, and he was pointing a finger at me. I said to a fellow,

"What's it say?"

"BRITONS, JOIN YOUR COUNTRY'S ARMY! GOD SAVE THE KING," he replied.

I ran home and said to my mother, "Lord Kitchener wants me to join the army."

"You are too young," she said, "But your father is signing on tomorrow." I felt proud that my father was joining the army to go to war, I couldn't wait to tell my mates, but their reply was the same, their fathers and older brothers were signing up too.

The next day, the 28th July 1914 there was a line of fine young men from the Town Hall to St Leonards Church, all chatting. There was an air of excitement as they waited to sign on for King and Country. Some older gents who had been in the Boer War stood proud, wearing their medals. A couple of days later off they went, most of them joining our local regiment, the South Staffordshire Regiment. They were young men, most of whom would never return.

At the outbreak of War in 1914, my father received his war papers and had to go to an army camp in Rugeley for training, following this he was sent to France. My father was one of the few to return, he was never the same, he returned a different man to the one that left us. I remember walking through the town, it was felt eerie quiet and empty, it must have been the same across the country, not many men folk around.

During my travels, I found my way to Brocton and Rugeley Army Camps, where the soldiers trained in readiness for the First World War. My father had already departed for the western front at this stage, so there was no hope of seeing him there. The government said the war would only last a few weeks, but Lord Kitchener told them it would last longer maybe three years. 'The war to end all wars,' they said.

It was a good walk for me twenty miles to the edge of Cannock Chase, I was very young, but I had an uncanny knack of getting to these places when I was playing truant from school. I once took a horse out of a stable in a field, one early morning, but more about that later. As time went on, I was getting into trouble for non-attendance at school. When I did go, my mother would drag me and say to the headmaster, Mr. Rhodes, 'give him the stick,' and when he went into his room to fetch it, I would *'bolt the course'* and go off on the road again. Often, I would be missing for two or three weeks at a time. I had a fascination of joining the army but still too young, I would sit for hours watching them march around the barracks doing musketry drill and watching the soldiers on horses, I couldn't wait to leave school and join up, but I was still only ten, the war would be over by the time I grew up.

The soldiers used to look after me until my mother was notified. When my mother called at the guardroom to collect me, I would say, "Never mind mother, I have got plenty of money to pay our fare back." The soldiers used to give me money for cleaning their buttons and boots, and fetching their papers. I would check the papers before taking them to the billets, to see if my absence from home was reported. I remember once in the local evening paper Express & Star, reading,

'Boy Wanderer Returns'

Local Magistrates warned that I would have to go to a Reformatory School, if I did not alter my ways.

Where I lived was not far from Bilston General Post Office, and the Town Hall which was then the Professor Woods Picture Palace. It was here on a Saturday afternoon that the children could go to the pictures for two pennies and on entry, each child would be given an apple or an orange. The other picture palace was the Electric Theatre, here you paid one penny, with each child receiving some sweets, so even in those days; there was competition. We would watch silent movies, Charlie Chaplin being a favourite, and just before the movie would start they would show us the news from the trenches.

When I was at home I would do errands for the people that lived in our street. These were some of the things I used to get; one penny of milk from Stokes on Swan Bank, two pennies of sugar, bruised fruit from Billingsbys in a basin, full already, for one penny and a quarter weight of coal '*28lb*' from a place called Whitehouse's, who were also the undertakers. Once playing hide and seek there, I fell asleep in a coffin. It was lined with purple velvet. The undertaker was situated at the back of the house and many a time we used to watch them making coffins. On collecting cheese and bread we used to ask for 'make weight', a slight bit of cheese that we took for ourselves, a small slice of Batch-Cake and a little piece of extra bread on top of our loaves that we carried from the bakehouse. Saturday mornings at about half past five I had to wait by the gas lamp on Swan Bank for a potato salesman with his horse and wagon. We used to go to the wholesaler's market in Wolverhampton where he would buy potatoes, vegetables and some fruit, then go around the streets selling his goods. Late at night when I had looked after his horse and they had closed the public house that he had been drinking till one in the morning, he would reward me with three pennies. This I had to take to my mother, along with a bag of bruised fruit.

On Easter or Whitsun holidays, it was a walk to Baggeridge Wood eight miles away. Our food for this great trip was a bottle of water, and some bread and dripping, and we were glad to pick apple cores up out of the gutter as we went along. On some Sunday mornings trips used to go from the local public houses. The conveyance consisted of two horses and a brake or wagonette, with a step on the back to allow passengers up on to it. The men used to say that twelve could get on, six either side. I could stand on the step because I was the horse minder. I looked after the horses while the men went in the boozer at the place they were going to; perhaps it might have been Wallheath Tavern or The Fox Tavern on the way to Bridgnorth. Sometimes after we had set off it used to pelt down with rain. The men didn't seem to mind because there was always a nine-gallon barrel of beer in the Brake, and many were sozzled before they got to their destination.

One day in 1917 we heard that a soldier from the South Staffordshire Regiment, a friend of my fathers who lived in Coseley, Bilston by the name of Private Thomas Barratt had been awarded the Victoria Cross at Ypres, Belgium, the citation read;

For most conspicuous bravery when as a scout to a patrol he worked his way towards the enemy line with the greatest gallantry and determination, despite continuous fire from hostile snipers at close range. When during the subsequent withdrawal of the patrol it was observed that a party of the enemy were endeavouring to out flank them, Private Barratt at once volunteered to cover the retirement, and this he succeeded in accomplishing. His accurate shooting caused many casualties to the enemy, and prevented their advance. Throughout the enterprise he was under heavy machine gun and rifle fire, and his splendid example of coolness and daring was beyond all praise. After safely regaining our lines, this very gallant soldier was killed by a shell.

The London Gazette 4th September 1917.

He was only twenty-two. It was such a shame that men like Thomas would never return, but I felt proud that our soldiers were doing brave deeds and even more so when Thomas was awarded the Victoria Cross. We also had another Victoria Cross awarded to Lance-Corporal George Onions, that's two from my small town.

Christmas was a big occasion for us in those days, to see what we had in our stockings. For instance, if we put our stockings on the bedrail and they had small holes in them, the first item put in would be *'gleeds'* which are small ashes, three or four chestnuts, six Spanish nuts, three or four, *'suck'*, which are sweet fishes, one apple and orange and a half new penny. The Christmas tree was two bowls brought in from outside, and a grape tub decorated with coloured paper with little chocolate mice, little sweet pigs, little chocolate cigars, hanging from it. That was our share just looking at these.

At Sunday morning breakfast we sat on the squab, a kind of old sofa, and if one of the family were working they had their meals on a plate along with a piece of bread dipped in tomato liquor. I remember quite well on a Saturday morning my mother went up to the back of the market and got me a pair of button up boots. She paid one shilling six pence for them. As I walked down the street the next day I knew that people were looking at me from behind their curtains. The best errand that I ever did was to take an old fellow his dinner each day to Sankey's Bankfield Works. The route was from the General Post Office *GPO* down Bath Street across a field, about a mile in distance. The dinner was potato, with meat on top in a basin, on top of the basin was a saucer or plate with bread. The whole lot was tied in what we called a Tommy handkerchief. Half way across the field I would untie the handkerchief and swipe the meat or sausage, no matter what it was he never got it, I used to eat it on my journey. No complaints were ever made and for my troubles I received three pennies per week.

Now I am ten years old, I became restless and decided to run away to Rugeley Camp, maybe I was envious, I wanted to be a part of this great adventure that they called a war. So, I decided it would be better to get away on horseback. For a week I slept in a stable which was situated in a field behind Harper's Brewery, now Edges Shoe factory in Bilston.

One morning I took a horse out of the stable, it was that big that to mount it I had to climb onto a cartwheel. I climbed on the spokes of the wheel onto the hub and then onto the top of the tyre, with the bridle and rope for reins I was on my way to Rugeley. On coming into Hednesford, I started to beg for bread and water for the horse and myself. I noticed a woman going to a house with the name 'POLICE' over the door, this is where the horse and myself parted company. A Detective Daniels questioned me about the horse; I denied all knowledge of ever seeing the horse. I thought I was getting away with it until he said,

"Harry take your trousers down."

I knew it was all over when he saw how red my posterior was.

He then said, "It's quite alright Harry we have found the horse."

Strangely I was not taken to court for this offence but sent to court for being out of control of my mother. I was placed in front of the local magistrate and sentenced to Industrial School until I was sixteen. I was escorted on a train to Stoke on Trent then walked the six miles with my suitcase escorted by a police officer up hill to the school. My escort said to me. "This is not like running off to Brocton is it?" I was young, I didn't see the seriousness in this I thought I would be home every evening, in fact I didn't return home for the next six years.

Chapter II

INDUSTRIAL SCHOOL

I was handed over with my committal papers to the governor a Mr Owen Braid. After saying,

"Look after yourself Harry," said the detective, as he left. I was on my own and this was going to be my home for the next six years. Industrial Schools were intended to solve problems of juvenile vagrancy, by removing poor and neglected children from their home environment to a boarding school. The school was split into houses. Each house had four prefects and a senior prefect, and a housemaster.

The time was now six o'clock, in the evening. After tea some of the boys played table tennis, whilst others read or played draughts, chess, dominoes and other games. I had got a bed for myself and a night-shirt. It was the end of a full day and I went to sleep, without thinking of home, as I never had been homesick. I was woken by the school bell at six-thirty in the morning. This bell was for a variety of reasons, as I learned later. The dormitory prefect shouted,

"Out of bed, all of you."

Out of bed I got and began to look around at the other boys who were making their beds. Each had a mattress, two white sheets, three blankets, a counterpane and a pillow. I was told that someone would show me how to make my bed. All the beds were made and put into uniformity. This I found was the first part of discipline. We filed down the stairs, and assembled in the day room where the register was called to see if all was present. If anyone absconded they would always be caught, be brought back and then suffer the consequences not just by the governor but by his pals as well. If one did abscond all the school were put on line. This meant all spare time was spent marching around in line, just like, being given exercise in a prison. All games, sport, forfeited, no talking allowed. My first breakfast consisted of porridge with salt and not sugar. Also bread and dripping. Before each meal, and after, we had to say grace. Another breakfast would be sausage and mash. Dinner was best. After all these years I can still remember the menu.

Monday,	Treacle pudding.
Tuesday,	Irish stew followed by rice pudding.
Wednesday,	Scotch broth.
Thursday,	Shepherd's pie.
Friday,	Cottage pie.
Saturday,	Steak and kidney pudding.
Sunday,	Steamed potatoes, with beef & Yorkshire pudding.

There was never much left in the dining hall. The boys in rotation took any extras. I soon got used to the knife, fork and spoon, no using fingers here. After my first breakfast I went for my medical inspection. Present was the matron, governor and medical officer. I had all my measurements taken, weight height, biceps, and head and foot measurements. She checked my hair for nits. She was so rough, she prized my mouth open to check my teeth before a final look down my earholes.

Chapter III

THE BIRCH

The school buildings stood on a hill approximately seven hundred feet above sea level and this was to be my home. Where people dreaded but where I found happiness as times went on.

Here I was on my own. A master and one the boys took charge of me. I was taken to have a bath, yes in a proper bath, different from the Saturday night in the rubbing tub on the hearth. Whilst I was bathing the boy gave me a good insight of school life. When I told him I was from Bilston, he told me that there were three other boys from my town here. After my bath I was fitted with a new set of clothes, consisting of trousers, jersey, shirt, undervest, pants, socks which turned down below the knees, boots for everyday wear, boots for Sundays, best suit, cap and cap badge and a blue cape, boot brushes and tooth brush along with these items my number, which was twenty-seven. This was to be my number for the duration of my stay at Werrington Industrial School about four miles East from Stoke on Trent.

I was taken into the governor's study; he was seated at a table with the matron a Miss Robertson. She was staring from the corner of the room. She resembled a Russian shot putter, with a scowl to match. She acted as mother to the inmates, one hundred and sixty boys from the ages ten to sixteen.

"Now my boy," he said.

"You are here for a long time and this is to be your home. You are the youngest and the smallest boy here so you will have to try to look after yourself, your number is twenty-seven and your house is called the Blues House."

The houses have a total of forty boys in each, Blues 1-40, Reds 41-80, Whites 81-120, and Greens 121-160. There were six dormitories, number six was for anyone that fouled the bed. I was put in number five. Trouble started right away a boy next to me, number twenty-six, same house as me, but bigger came up to me like a bantam cock. He looked me all over, walked around me, tapped me on the chest chanting,

"1,2,3, I am cock of thee, if thee hits me, I'll hit thee," bump, he punched on the chin and strutted away. I was lost and my battle for life had begun. I had to defend myself for there was another one hundred and fifty-nine boys in the school. One of the chaps from my hometown had heard what had happened. He was aged about thirteen and he gave me some advice. He said be prepared, the same thing will happen again. If anyone comes and starts before he says three hit him on the chin and hope for the best. It was not long before another chap came up and on the same hop before he could say three, I hit him with such a ferocious punch hoping no retribution would fall upon me. That sent my prestige about twelve up in the ranks.

* * * * * * * *

The whole school was situated in about one hundred acres of land and comprised the following, dormitories, recreation or day-room, four classrooms, gymnasium and band room. Boiler house, woodwork and metalwork rooms, dining room, sickbay, officer's kitchen and cookhouse, needle and sewing rooms, washhouses and bathroom. Swimming baths, kitchen, gardens and the farm that included three horses, ten cows and calves, poultry, eight pigs, and about sixty acres of farmland. If on attaining thirteen years of age one thought of making farming a career he could go on the school farm. The daily tasks were milking, driving, ploughing, haymaking, and dairying. I enjoyed working on the farm. At sixteen, these farm hands if approved by the Home Office could work on farms approved by the authorities. A Mr Holdcroft who was the bailiff and Mr Wainwright who was the foreman managed our farm. Mr Grey looked after the kitchen garden. Our water supply was a spring situated about a mile away. Every morning a group of us with buckets would fill them up and take them back to the kitchens. This was done every day in all weathers you dare not spill a drop. Good workers from here went out to places like Keele Hall, now Keele University.

One officer and one woman staffed the laundry, with six boys; here all the school's laundry was done. Fixed on one of the walls as you entered this building was the dreaded birch rod. I will tell you later how I had the birch administrated to me. The kitchen and cookhouse ran by an officer and eight boys. Sewing and darning was done and all repairs to clothing. Here I learnt to sew and knit. Boot repairs were sent to the cobblers. Any dental treatment we were sent to Hanley, four miles away we had to walk there and back. We liked a walk away from the school, we could get a smoke of course. The favourite place was the gym, also in here the band used to practice. I had the occasion to be a learner in the band on the Clarinet, many was the time that I had a good clip around the ear by our headmaster Mr Barber, for playing off by heart instead of reading music. He was also the physical training instructor. He was a fine man. One year I was champion of gym. I owe him and the school for the physical condition I have always been in during my life. One of my former pals became bandmaster of a famous army regiment. I can still remember nearly all the officers' names and the boys with their numbers. These were the days when real punishment was handed out for various offences.

I have mentioned the birch. The stick was always given on the backside and never on the hands. If anyone was reported for obscene language they had their mouth scrubbed out with a small brush and carbolic soap.

We boasted a lovely library and debating societies. Political and historical scholars gave speeches, we had sports days. The school had a great football and cricket team we played matches at home and away with civilian teams. In fact, about twelve men and four women and one hundred and sixty boys ran the whole place. Now I have given you a good insight of the school I will now carry on with my boyhood days there. As the days rolled by me I was getting to know all the do's and don'ts and even then, being very young as I was, I seemed to have a gift in knowing things in general.

I was always a lone wolf but I had to team up with someone, this ruled out twenty-six Ward but twenty-eight Thorpe was a decent chap. He came from Derby; he used to have parcels sent from home. He always gave me some sweets and biscuits. He slept in the bed next to me; above all he was a good athlete. Until you reached twelve you went to school full time. This was all right for me until I got fed up. When I was ten I had the idea in my head to run away. I had often been told that you could not get any further than the church or a mile radius of the school. I thought I could beat this and build on my reputation within the school.

One day I was being shown how to darn socks by the needlewoman with a group of other boys. We had a fifteen-minute break, five minutes before the break I asked permission to leave the room. This gave me a twenty-minute start. My route took me over farmers' fields through country lanes, constantly looking for stone markers with arrows pointing towards Stoke. Eventually I made my way to the goods entrance of the railway station and looked at the tallies on the trucks to see where they were going to. I looked for Bilston but I noticed some were going to Wolverhampton. I climbed into one of the trucks and it was not long before I was on my way home. This was the opposite of what I had been used to, I had always run away from home, now I was running back. I finally arrived at Bilston. My liberty was of a short duration, for waiting at the bottom of the street where I lived, was Sgt Cartwright and Detective Daniels. At six o'clock an officer from the school reported at the police station to take me back. I didn't even have time to say hello to my mother. Getting back late at night did not give the other boys much time to settle. They had to suffer during my absence. At nine o'clock the following morning, the whole school assembled in the large classroom, one hundred and sixty boys, masters and the governor Mr Braid. I have never been so humiliated in all my life. No reason was asked of me why I had absconded. If I had to have the birch at a police court there would have only been an inspector, policeman and doctor in attendance. Here was this big audience and no doctor. I should have had six strokes with the birch but by the time the governor had finished I had thirteen. As the governor was about to give me the first stroke I was timid and I would say, 'on there,' pointing to where I wanted it. The birch was given first, off with your jersey, trousers dropped down, shirt lifted, you bend down leaving your backside bare and the birch is then laid on this. Before the birch was put in use it was kept soaked in linseed oil for a period. I was put to bed and for three days I was picking thorns out of my backside. The matron used to come and visit me. The treatment of the birch cured me at least for a year or two. As time went on I settled down and unexpectedly I was beginning to enjoy school life. I was putting on weight, I had good food and cod liver oil and malt.

Visits by your parents were allowed on condition that you had been on good behaviour and I shall never forget the first call from my mother. She could not believe her eyes when she came to see me for the first time. It was not only, noticeable in my appearance but in my manners and speech. It came as a great shock to her when I said words as, please, thank you, beg your pardon, or if you don't mind. On one visit I could sense that there was something wrong. She told me that my eldest sister Hannah who we called Nancy had emigrated with her husband Albert Humpage to America to start a new life after seeing an advertisement in the Express & Star, looking for canal boatmen and coal miners she sailed on the cruiser RMS Cedric with Albert to New York from Liverpool settling in Ladd, Illinois about one hundred miles West of Chicago, just North of the

Illinois River and next to Blackball Mines. Joseph Owen went a few months prior to Nancy where he settled for the rest of his life. Albert Humpage blew himself up in his backyard whilst making moonshine at the time of the prohibition. Nancy's son only five at the time saw his father running out head to toe in flames. Once Nancy had settled I remember my mother telling me she had received a letter from her asking for me to go over there, I was only fourteen at the time and even though my mother was struggling bringing up the family she wouldn't let me go. Anyhow my mother was seeing me progress here at the Industrial School and couldn't bear the thought that two of her children had gone to America. I have fond memories of my sister she was my half-sister the daughter of Joseph Owen she was six years older than me she helped my mother look after me when I became a handful. I never saw my sister again, no technology in those days just a pen and some paper. I corresponded with my sister Nancy over the years she passed away in 1968.

The things I played truant for at school as they didn't seem right for my education were being shown to me in a different light. Gone was the old way of teaching different subjects. I was one of the first in the country to come under what was called the Dalton Plan. It was an educational concept created by Helen Parkhurst, her aim was to achieve a balance between a child's talent and the needs of the community. I believe that it started in America. The plan was this, all your education subjects were tabulated together. Say you were given one month to finish these lessons, and completed them in three weeks, then the remaining week could be optional spent on your favourite subjects that were not in your plan. My time used to be spent in all sport records. I was good at history, politics, dramatics and poetry. This made me popular, as different groups would want me in their quiz teams and other groups. I am still quite good in these subjects today. I resolved to settle down because by now I only had another a couple of years left at the school. I was well away in the field of sport and was jolly when my name went on our house notice board that I had been selected to play football at outside left for my house blues against the greens. I had become a permanent team member and my ambition was to play for my school. I liked football and with my fitness from my gym work, my ambition was to play one day for Wolverhampton Wanderers, my local football team. They won the FA Cup the year I was born. This year 1924 they got promoted to the second division, that pleased my Stoke mates as our teams would be playing each other.

I was now doing a lot of reading and learning poetry. Do not think because I was swotting like this that I was a goody-goody, I was still up for some tomfoolery. I liked poetry because I used to live only one hundred yards from a great English poet's birthplace, Sir Henry Newbolt. When I used to read poetry I often thought to myself, one day I shall be a poet. Sunday, we all went to church and our band used to play as we marched to the church and if it was fine, crowds used to come from miles around to watch us. I joined the choir, not because I could sing, but to have the job of organ blower. The organ was a wind instrument and air had to be pumped into it. Another boy and myself used to do this job during the service, and of course we could snatch a draw on a cigarette, without being seen by anyone. We could get the cigarettes from one of the members of the civilian choir. Choir practice used to be on Thursday evenings, we were then entrusted to make our own way to the church. After church three times a week for seven years I got fed up with it and although I say it I think too much religion in the way can turn one as it did to me. When I was thirteen I was confirmed by the Bishop of Lichfield in the church. The time came when I was made prefect by now I was getting along nicely, well behaved, good sportsman, a gift in different subjects and could converse about things with the best. One night each week my house master would teach a history class about happenings in the Great War (1914-1918). He could hold us entranced for about ten minutes and then he would say twenty-seven come out to the front and continue for the next five minutes. I would carry on making it up myself. I enjoyed this. I had got out of talking Black Country dialect some time ago, only reverting to it on occasions like this.

The main thing in all our minds was always visiting day when our parents would always bring us parcels, cake, sweets, fruit in fact everything that boys looked forward to. They were allowed two hours at the school and we could show them all over the school. The best day for this would-be Whit Monday this was our sports day and there was the keenest of competition for the house championship. Our house was always near the top of the table championship. At the age of fifteen I was school champion at sports. I was made senior prefect and captain of the school.

We visited other reformatory schools and played them at cricket and football. Being interested in sport, dramatic art and Shakespearean plays I had the greatest privilege of meeting or seeing the following; Championship of Europe fifteen rounds Boxer Tommy Harrison *Haney* and Charles Leduave of France. Harold Abrahams, Eric Liddell *Scotch flyer*. Howard Baker, Sam Carroll, *High Jumpers*. Earl Thompson *Canadian hurdler*. Abrahams, I believe cleared over twenty-four feet in long jump and was immortalised in the film, Chariots of Fire. Liddell one hundred yards 9.9 secs. Thompson, *Hurdles*. Baker played goal for Chelsea. Helen Terry, Arnold Bennett, Henry Ainley from the Shakespearean stage.

We were all used to silence, but the greatest silence that I ever experienced was the Armistice Day of November 11th, 1918. I was playing on the school farm with the two horses, Dolly & Tommy when the hooters went at eleven o'clock everything was still and quiet, not even a bird twittered there was peace at last in the world. I stood silent and thought about the soldiers I had the pleasure of meeting at Cannock and Rugeley army camps and wondered if any had survived or perished at the Somme. It was the end of the Great War, the war to end all wars. If only I knew then what was going to happen later in my life. A few days later they took us to Stoke-on-Trent to see the soldiers marching through the city, flags flying, people cheering but the soldiers looked sad, maybe from the horrors they had witnessed. A few weeks later there was resentment between the soldiers and the politicians who had sent them to war, was it worth the cost of so many lives?

* * * * * * * *

I was fortunate to have a little training on the farm and I was at home with the horses. The first job I had was scarecrow minding. In the fields were scarecrows an old mannequin dressed as a man. A little breeze blows clothes about, keeps crows off the seeds. If this fails you are armed with a rattle, you can twist this and it rattles scaring the crows and other birds away. I was then cow minding seeing that the cows didn't break through the hedges. Morning and night, I helped with the milking and when a cow had calved the first lot of milk it was called beestings, this was given to the cooks who made 'Beestings Pudding' for the farm hands. I remember one day the governor went around the poultry farm and found a cockerel with his head off. It was proved that the poultry farm boy had knocked his head off with a sweeping brush. His punishment was he had to walk about with the cockerel's head and a card round his neck stating, 'I knocked his head off.' This punishment lasted all week.

There used to be a fair number of fights amongst the boys, but they were always the best of friends once they settled their differences. For all the experience that I had of the farm work, which was I could milk cows, look after and work horses grooming and ploughing I did not fancy the idea of going to work for other farmers, for I had seen too many boys come back, for some had to work too hard, were ill-treated and used as cheap labour.

In due course the governor left and our senior housemaster Mr JD Johnstone was the new governor. He took over the time that the first flu epidemic started, around about 1920. The epidemic killed 228,000 people, it is thought it had been spread by the soldiers returning from the trenches in Northern France. He was the finest governor anyone could have. A third of the school were confined to bed in our different dormitories, later there were about one hundred boys down at the same time. JD and his wife and the matron did yeoman service in attending to the patients. Recovery was swift and doctors first called it the 'three-day fever.' In those days there were no television, and radio was a small contraption, you used to get your station with what you called the 'Cat's Whisker.' Papers were sent to me each week and I would receive them on Monday mornings. The previous weeks-nightly Express & Star and Saturday night's Sporting Star. These were always greatly looked forward to. Sometimes when a new boy arrived, it was my job to show him the ropes and as they were always homesick and heartbroken, it was not an easy job getting them settled in.

Once a week in the summer we used to go for walks in small groups round the country lanes, here we had secret rendezvous with the girls of the different villages. They would bring us sweets and cigarettes. Woodbines were only two pennies for five. The village church always had a good congregation of these girls for it was here that notes and letters were passed on. Being a member of the dramatic society passed the winter nights, debating and Shakespearean plays, I have taken part in plays. On occasions we went to the Grand Hanley. It was here that I had the great pleasure of meeting Dame Helen Terry, Arnold Bennett, Henry Ainley. I put Bilston on the map when I told my pals that Sir Henry Newbolt the poet was born there. I used to recite his poem 'Play up & Play the Game.' Also, that Tom Webster the Worlds famous cartoonist came from here.

I had two holidays each year from school, I often encountered a sense of jealousy among my former friends the reason being my speech and accent had greatly improved and they thought that I was putting it on. My knowledge of the world had broadened out, but it was only my education that I was getting here that seemed to put me ahead of my pals. As time passed on it was beginning to dawn on me that I would be sorry for when I should have to leave all my friends from the governor down to the latest intake and all the interest in all life that I had.

Chapter IV

LEAVING SCHOOL

On the morning of my release on my sixteenth birthday, I broke down and cried, for the second time in my life. I had got to face this world on my own. Each boy leaving school was clothed with two new suits, two pairs of boots, two shirts, two undervests, two pair's underpants, and two pairs of socks. The governor dropped me off in his car at the station. I caught the train at Stoke and roughly two hours later I was at home. I left on a Saturday from my old school. On Monday I started work at a moulding foundry as a 'Sand Riddler.' My elder brother got me this job. In this job I had to keep six moulders going all day, by mixing sand with a shovel, moving the weights off one mould on to another whilst they were casting. After casting tipping the moulds over, knocking out the castings and mixing the sand up again. After sticking at this job for about six months I got a job at a haulage firm, working at a slag firm, 'tar slag,' which had just started up. The place that I worked had about sixty horses. Both the horses and myself worked two six-hour shifts per day twelve hours in total. I used to get to the stables at 0530, report at the slag works by 0600, and work right through till midday, for a bite to eat, then 1300 till 1900 hours, for this I received the sum of thirty-six shillings per week. I next worked a three-horse team with a wagon, taking steel strip to different works. I still could not get on with my family and friends. I think it was because I always appeared to be a lone wolf. After days of pondering this I decided to leave home and go on the road tramping.

Chapter V

GENTLEMAN TRAMP

One day without telling my parents I left home and started on the road. This is where one could move from county to county helping on farms or doing manual labour on building sites. Now being fresh at this new kind of life I thought I would learn all the tricks of the trade. So, I began by kipping at the lodging houses. Here I could get a night's kip for eight pennies. I soon found out that you had to have your wits about you in these places for these places were packed each night and day with thieves and ne'er- do- wells. I have been in these lodging houses when they have been packed out especially on Friday nights when now and again you would get a tramp drop in, by doing this he would be clear of the spike, 'Casual Ward' for the end of the week. One of these lodging houses that I often frequented was in Britannia Street, Leicester. Here I met a fellow by the name of Yorky, notably from Yorkshire. From him I learned a lot of information about the road. After gleaning information from him I decided it was time that I started tramping myself as by now nearly all my money had gone. This morning I started on this carefree life, but I think that I was a bit different from the ordinary tramp. I carried my own razor, boot brushes, towel and soap. The first day I covered about twenty miles, all on foot. On entering the first spike that I ever went in it was quite different to what I expected soon as I entered reception, an orderly looked me up and down and eventually asked me if I had come to the right place. I told him my story and he asked me what casual ward was my next call, I have told him that I had come out of a lodging house that morning. I found out that if one should get complete alibis always, it is best to always give your correct name, what spike you have come from and what spike you are bound for. I relate this instance. I was coming out of the spike at Northampton one Wednesday morning when two policemen apprehended me and took me to the police station and questioned to where I had been, my home, and where I had stayed. They must have enquired to see if I was telling the truth. It transpired the police were after a man named Furniss who was later caught and hanged for murder. I believe that he set fire to a hut that he had for an office with a man inside, a tramp if I remember right. I think he did it for life insurance money. The tramps body although unrecognisable was purported to be his own. Now when one meets a tramp they think are dirty and scruffy, but on entering each casual ward, they are given a bath and their clothes are fumigated and off to bed. Next day you do a day's work, wood chopping, manual labour. And all next morning you leave at nine o'clock taking with you a wrapped sandwich. I soon got all my utensils, which every tramp carries. One 'drumming up' tin, which is usually a large loose snuff tin, piece of inner tubing. Food on the road didn't cost a lot, three pennies for bits of meat, potatoes and vegetables out of any farmer's field for free. Clean water you could always get by looking for the embers of a tramp's fire, you knew that water was handy, a little stream nearby, for no tramp lights a fire without there being water for cooking and brewing up. First, out comes our inner tube, pick a few twigs, light a fire, put tin containing meat on fire, prepare spuds, add when meat is done, have meal, swill tin out, make your tea. In about another three hours' time I shall be making my way to the next spike admittance it would be at six o'clock in the evening. By now I knew that each spike had its own tramp major. There were crafty fingers, having been once on the road, perhaps on entering they had feigned illness been put in casual sick quarters and made the place their own. They knew all the gossip, and on entering if you had any cigarettes, give him some and you were made eventually, he would sell these at cut price to the old inmates not tramps, who were resident there. If you go into a casual ward on a Friday night, you were not allowed out again until Monday morning, so to pass the time away, I used to read the tarot cards to some of the tramps. I made their predictions up. One tramp I told his fortune to must have been guilty of what I had told him, for I found out on the Monday morning just before I came out as I was washing my outfit that someone had 'nicked' my soap. Right away the fellow offered to lend me his soap, which I accepted. Now the ordinary tramp would have straight away started to rinse and lather his face, but not me. My way of washing was to rinse and lather my hands and arms first. On rubbing the soap between my hands, I cut my hands to pieces, if I had washed my face first like others, my face would have been in a pretty mess. He had fixed a razor blade in the soap that he had loaned me. At different casual wards by listening to other tramp's conversations I got to know where one could call at on the road and get a few 'fags' and a 'mashing' of tea. I also got to know where the places you had got to steer clear of. One of the real gentlemen that I numbered among my friends was a Mr Frank Gray, who was a MP for one of the constituencies of Oxford. I believe he was a Liberal and welfare campaigner, he was once a solicitor and when the Great War broke out he refused a commission to serve as a private soldier. I made it my business to call at his place. I think that it was Kidlington near Oxford, I knocked at the door of the big house. A maid opened the door. On asking my business, I told her that I wished to see Mr Gray, as I was a 'Knight' of the road, she looked me up and down, noticing that my boots were clean, that I wore a collar and tie and wore no cap, and my hair parted, she could hardly believe what I had told her. She told me that he was not in, but she would tell Mrs Gray, after five minutes, Mrs Gray came spoke to me and believe it or not I was invited in. After a while Frank Gray returned home, and he was just what the fraternity said he was. It turned out that he was the champion of the wayfarer. He had even asked questions in Parliament for the better treatment of tramps in the casual wards, and so that he could verify everything that he had stated in the house he accompanied me for three weeks on the road. He lived the same as me, no favours, no extras, and just a tramp. At the end I was recompensed generously by Frank. Years later, when I was a Sergeant in the Glider Pilot Regiment, some of our pilots were training at Kidlington, I travelled down there to see them and visit Frank Gray, but I could not find Frank I was told he had passed away in 1935.

At times if I had a 'skipper,' to say sleep out under a hedge or in a barn, I found that a drop of mentholated spirits would keep one warm. This was the only time that I drink this 'stuff.' It would put you out for about six hours, you would sleep; of course, you would not feel the cold once you were asleep. I have often seen tramps half-mad after drinking lots of this 'stuff.' I have never met a tramp and his proper wife, but of course there are casual wards for women. Mind you they can team up when they are pea picking, potato picking, sugar beet pulling or hop picking. They would be together and 'kip' out together until these seasons were finished. There has always been 'knights of the road', the most famous of these being The Highway Robbers, Jonathan Wild from Wolverhampton, and the famous Dick Turpin. Turpin and Wilde were beheaded in Newgate Gaol.

Chapter VI

JOINING THE ARMY

On coming back home, I found that there was no work to be had. I even went to the extent of answering a newspaper article that appeared in the local newspaper, Express and Star, on why was it that people could not get males to do domestic service. I wrote to the paper and was fixed up for an interview with Mrs Lloyd Davies, wife of a Wolverhampton doctor. I told her my story of the past and strangely enough, I got the job, but when it came to tell me about what clothes I had to wear, I could not tell the lady that my mother could not afford to buy me new clothes. I have often wondered if this lady and the local paper thought that I was a 'crank.' It was at this time I went on two or three occasions to enlist in the army but I was turned down because I was not tall enough, I was an inch too short. Eventually I was accepted and became 4910683 Pte H Owen, in the South Staffordshire Regiment with the large number of shillings per day.

I was soon to find out that the soldiering I had to get used to was nothing like my escapades as a boy. I have always had a schedule for doing things on different days of the week. Being keen on sport, I soon found out that I was about the best in athletics in my squad and used to look forward to my PT in the gym every morning. On Wednesday afternoons we used to have cross country runs and many a time that two pals and myself have finished up at my home for cigarettes and food that my mother would give us. We always arrived back at our billets at night. The army in my time, early 1920's was not like it is today. In those days you could not talk about politics in the barrack room, you could not write to your MP expressing any political opinion otherwise you were classed as a 'Bolshie,' and you were never in favour with NCO's and Officers. The day came when it was time for us to join our battalion and it was good for we had become full-blown soldiers. I left the depot having gained my second-class certificate of education. My previous schooling having stood me in good stead. When I joined my battalion many people in my town knew of my past and of course it played on my mind to think that they were talking about me. Soldiering came easy to me and I was useful at sport, but for all this I seemed to be troubled and could not get settled. I was stationed at Folkestone, Kent and had the pleasure of seeing many people training for attempts to swim the channel. I once met Dr Logan and Harry Carey her coach, a woman who received £1000 for swimming the channel and then returned the money, saying she had not swam it stating a channel swim could be fixed. I believe that this was the sum and the 'News of the World', paper gave her the money. It was at Hythe that I again met Dame Helen Terry, she was nearing ninety now. I was on a course for riding, driving and grooming, at the 42nd Battery, 2nd Field Brigade Royal Artillery. I passed with a ninety-three percent record. On my return to my regiment I got the job as 'Batman Groom,' to the company commander. My captain should have paid me twenty shillings per month, I never got it, so I had an interview with the company commander, he wasn't amused that I had the audacity to complain about one of his officers so I was moved to Head Quarters Transport Section. Here I oversaw Mules and Limber Wagons; which are two wheeled carts this was too much for my pride. My dress in these days was jacket, puttees, spurs, lanyard and riding crop. Even though I enjoyed working with horses and I was very good at it, I needed a challenge, some adventure in my life!

Chapter VII

ON THE RUN

Add to the love of adventure after a weekend leave, I didn't return to the barracks. I was on the run for five weeks, of course, I was listed as a deserter. I was sitting in the local picture palace one afternoon; there were silent pictures in those days. Suddenly flashed on the screen were the words, 'Will Private H Owen report to the Pay Box.' No pay box for me, I made my exit through another door, collected my civvies and case and was off again. Oh, the military police were waiting for me; I put in good many miles that night and arrived at Victoria Station. There were many military police on the station, so I went into the toilets as a soldier, and came out a civvy, it was easy, I dumped my army gear in the toilets. After wandering about London for a couple of weeks, I was picked up by the police. I had to await military escort. On arriving back to my regiment, I was confined to the guardroom. Here I was awarded, note the term, 'A District Court Martial.' I elected to defend myself, I was charged with desertion and loss of kit. This had been purloined by my mates whilst I was on the run.

Chapter VIII

GLASSHOUSE

I had not got much of a chance and I was awarded one hundred and twelve days detention in the dreaded 'Glass House' at Aldershot, what you would call a military detention centre. A glasshouse is a military prison first established in 1844. Aldershot where I was imprisoned was the first one and because of its glazed roof got the nickname the Glasshouse. When I went to the Glasshouse, I had to have new kit, as in those days a soldier's kit comprised of eighty-four articles. Everything was done at the double, except for musketry and arms drill. Pack drill was the hardest.

Your valise pack contained your ammo boots, service dress, one shirt, holdall with contents socks and ground-sheets, webbing equipment, rifle and bayonet. This was heart-breaking for a young infantryman drilling with guardsmen, doing the same punishment. It was a harsh regime.

The corrective training started from basic military training much like recruit training. Fitness to the highest level ready for re-introduction back to your regiment. In some cases you could be discharged from the army once serving your sentence. When I came out, I was a sent back to my regiment, a full-blown soldier, fitter than when I left, but sadly in debt. For weeks, my pay was only one shilling per week. I used to parade, my name was called out by the company quarter master, like this, "4910683 Private Owen H," I would reply, "Sir," march up, salute, the CQMS would say to the paying out officer, "one shilling sir," but now and again he would say, "four pennies stoppages for regimental haircut." The officer would then give me eight pennies. On a Saturday, I would go out with about thirty shillings in my pocket.

Each Saturday there was a commanding officers parade, all webbing equipment had to be cleaned, sparkling and brasses polished. My platoon mates used to go out on Friday's so they would give me one shilling each to clean their brasses ready for the commanding officer's inspection the next day. As a matter of fact, I used to be quite rich and I was far better off than those on fourteen shilling per week.

Life started to get better for me and eventually I played cricket, football and hockey for my battalion. The time was looming for when we should go abroad, but one outstanding parade that I was on was when

Prince George aged nineteen, was opening a new wing at Folkestone Hospital, I was part of the Guard of Honour.

Chapter IX

MALTA

By now we were preparing to travel to Malta, having inoculations, being fitted with overseas kit. The time could not come quick enough for me, as I was waiting to see what soldiering abroad was like. I had never left England. Our battalion strength was in the region of eight hundred officers and men. One morning at 4.30am the battalion paraded and we marched to Folkestone railway station and our band played as we marched. At that early hour thousands of people turned out to see us depart on the train to Southampton. On arriving at Southampton, we embarked on the troop ship HMS Neuralia which was previously used as a hospital ship in the Great War and carried thousands of troops out East. We were seen off by our Colonel in Chief, Sir Charles Tucker, who was well respected in the battalion seeing action in the Zulu war and who later became a Lieutenant General, as the band on the quayside played 'Homeland,' we set sail for Malta, it was the year 1928.

The vessel was crammed with 1,200 men, cooped up packed in bunks trying to find a bit of space for yourself and your kit. We didn't waste much time on every mess deck we got out the cards and dominoes, banter was at full swing and we spent the evenings out on top deck star gazing. People pointing out the different constellations. I used to think if my mother could see me now out on the blue ocean, sun shining, getting a tan, in the fresh air, no Black Country smog out here.

I shall now mention one of my pals, by the name of Andrews from Grimsby, who we called 'Sinbad.' He had worked on Tramp Steamers and said that he was a 'Trimmer,' someone who moves coal around a ship for the engines. We kidded the corporal in charge of our mess deck to make him mess orderly; this entailed his duties to bring out meals from the galley, Sinbad was pleased; he would fetch our food for our table twenty-four. For three whole days he tripped up and down the stairs, no boots on, trousers turned up. We were now sailing through the notorious Bay of Biscay and we were all feeling rather seasick. On the fourth day, Sinbad winded his way towards the galley for the usual mornings breakfast of kippers. He had an unsteady gait, and he looked pale and ghastly, we knew quite well that it would not be long before he would be down with seasickness. The

South Wales Borderers, whose mascot was a goat, quartered opposite, in the cook's galley. Previously Sinbad had told me about this goat, but we had taken it with a pinch of salt. Half an hour had gone by, and Sinbad had not returned, so I was detailed to go and look for him and I did not feel too good myself. Every time that I think of the sight that met my eyes, I have a good laugh. The goat was there all right, and opposite him, divided by a truss of hay was Sinbad rocking and rolling, holding the tray of kippers and being sick! I don't know who looked the most objected, Sinbad, or the goat.

I informed the corporal in charge about Sinbad's malaise although he could tell by the state of the breakfast. Half of our mess was conked out and so were many more hundreds of the ships company who were lying about feeling ill. The weather in the next two days became quite warm and on the night of the sixth day in the distance we could see the lights of Valetta. The following morning, we dropped anchor. Troops on the top deck looked at the majestic sight of the Maltese shoreline. The first thing that struck me was the heat, I had never experienced anything so warm. I was sweating profusely and I hadn't even done anything physical. They said we had to acclimatize to the heat. The guys who had served out in India said it was even worse there, very humid. It was the first time most of us had left Great Britain, a few of the senior ranks had been to the Far East. By now everyone was waiting to see what the island of Malta had to offer. For myself I was more than excited, for I knew a little of the history of Malta. On disembarking, our company had the barracks at St Andrews. After two days of settling down I paid a visit to the tattooist who practised in a gully down at St Julian's Bay and straight away I entered into a contract with him. This was that if he put a tattoo on me for nothing then I would bring him customers from my regiment also paying me commission for each tattoo that he put on them. I have many tattoos on my body today, I have never regretted having them. I have steered clear of serious illnesses and infections. The culture and customs that we do in our country are quite different to what people do on these islands and countries in the Middle East or Far East. For instance, what a sight to behold, about twenty goats stop outside a house and some fellow milks one of them, into a glass. Then moves onto the next house. The strangest thing that I believe any service man has seen in Malta was what we called the Munje Waller. A Maltese businessman takes on a contract with the PRI shop *'President Regimental Institute'* to clear all dining room tables, he pays for this contract. All scraps of food are collected by Maltese and put in tins. These are then carried out of the barracks into some side street or road. Maltese men then queued up and for one half penny could dip in the tin and have a handful of food. If they had any paper with them, they had twice the amount for one penny. This they ate on the spot. It was said that underneath Valletta itself there were storerooms with enough food to last a siege or famine for seven years. One of the chief guard duties that I did there was at the Governors Palace. Sir John Philip Du Cane Count was the governor and Commander in Chief at the time. The Prime Minister was Lord Strickland, Count Della Catena. Malta is well known for its catacombs. The story goes that long ago a teacher took a party of school children down there one day and that they were never seen again. There were places like Valetta, Sliema, Msida and Floriana with plenty of interesting sights, Malta is well known for its lace making.

* * * * * * * *

Football and Cricket was the entertainment for the troops and Bingo which was played by all on the island. Our drinking and dining places were down Strada Stretta. The main drinking song, sung by everybody was:

We are two Irish Maltese.
We come from the island of Malta.
The first time we met was down Strada Strett.
We are two Irish Maltese.

Many men worked on the docks and one of the finest sights to see was the fleet coming in and out on exercise. It was while I was stationed here that I encountered one of the first players ever to get suspended in English Football. His name was Barney Travers. I believe he played for Fulham at the time, he tried to bribe the South Shields full back in the English cup-tie. He was acting as coach to one of the continental teams. Tottenham Hotspur came out to the island and played four or five matches. Whilst stationed here I had the odd occasion to visit Gozo a small island three or four miles away. Not many inhabitants here but they are Maltese, another island opposite Malta was the Kemmuna Islands, this place was used to be a quarantine base. Malta itself is nearly all-Catholic denomination. Most of our time was spent swimming either in St Georges Bay or at St Julian's Bay. Football, hockey and polo were played on the Marsa, a fine sports field.

Chapter X

PALESTINE

The day came when we had to embark for Palestine, this was a time when the Arabs and Jews were fighting each other. We were sent to assist in the repression of Arab terrorists. There had been much rioting and many deaths between the Arabs and Jews. We heard that British police who had been stationed there were overwhelmed with the disorder and riots. On one instance the police fired onto an Arab crowd to ward off an attack, killing many locals. So, one afternoon in 1929 we embarked on HMS Courageous. This had been decommissioned after the first world war then rebuilt as an aircraft carrier during the mid-1920's. She could carry forty-eight aircraft. This was the same carrier to be sunk by the Germans in 1939 at the beginning of the Second World War. It did not take long for us to reach Palestine from Malta, about five days at sea.

When we arrived at Jaffa, Tel Aviv we had to disembark into small boats as there was no quayside at Jaffa. A tugboat towed us then about fifty yards from land we had to wade through water, waist deep over rocks to reach the beachhead where trucks were waiting for us. Our destination was to be Haifa, north of where we had landed. Other British troops stationed in the Middle East had also been sent to the Holy Land. Palestine was a mandated territory, which had been given to us to protect after the Great War. It was 1917 that Field Marshal Viscount Allenby nicknamed, The Bull, had chased the Turks out of Jaffa and Jerusalem and in 1918 went on to capture northern Palestine, therefore, she came under our protection. The Arabs and Jews had started a little war of their own. One side thought that we had gone to protect them and the other side vice versa.

This was supposed to be land flowing with milk and honey, things that I had been told when I was young, but the only thing that I saw was desert and rock another place that I was soon to walk on foot.

On arriving at Hebron our transport was driven by Arabs, a strange sight met our eyes; Jews had been slaughtered and thrown into open graves. We later found out this was known as the Hebron massacre, the killing of about seventy Jews. We eventually restored order. Jews say that Palestine, Israel belonged to them but the Arabs were saying it was theirs. Palestine had her own police corps comprising of both Arab and Jews. The Arabs lived in their own towns and villages and the Jews in their colonies. On the borders lived the dreaded Bedouins who used to raid different villages; they rode horses and camels. The working of the Arabs outside of Tel Aviv and Jaffa were in the Orange Groves owned by the Jews. I have known the Arabs walk ten miles to work in these groves for ten shekel a day. In their villages they had no sanitation facilities and having no recreation, it was a poor life. The weapons used on skirmishes between the Arabs and Jews were rifles, revolvers and other weapons left behind by the Germans and Turks when they fled Palestine in 1917. It was here that I witnessed a kind of torture that I had never seen before. Certain leaders had fled to different villages when they knew that English soldiers were on their heels. One day I was sent with an Arab policeman to one of the villages to bring in a certain leader. We got him and proceeded by donkey to a courthouse. On entering the courthouse, a strange sight met my eyes. Arabs were in the courtyard running around in single file, while two Palestine policemen were holding a rifle, horizontal position. One holding the butt end the other grabbing the muzzle end and in between the sling and rifle were the soles of an Arabs feet. The rifle was lifted until the Arabs body was in the air and resting on his head. The police then wailed on his soles of his feet with leather coshes or sticks. In this way they soon answered questions that were put to them. I believe that this was the only way that you could get these Arabs to talk. This way you could get the truth out of them. After a while, law and order was established in this country, the Jews made accusations that their people had been mutilated and murdered by the Arabs and thrown into mass graves. An inquiry commission was sent to Palestine from England to investigate these charges. I was present on one of these examinations, wearing a respirator because the smell at the graveside was terrible. A grave was opened; there were about sixty-three bodies, men and women dumped by a roadside. The commission found no mutilation but I reserve my own comments on this.

Eventually after doing various duties at Hefa, Halbus, Safed and Safrafen we had to do a tour of duty at Tel Aviv. This was quite westernised, where both Arabs and Jews lived. I was learning Hebrew quite well, which would come in handy for a later escapade of mine, but also to converse with the locals. It was part of hearts and minds and it looked good for the locals to see we were trying.

You can trust the British soldier to look after himself in foreign countries and I have resorted to some tricks in my time, of which I have many good memories. One of occasions was at Mount Carmel which is a coastal mountain range in northern Israel, stretching from the Mediterranean. One night whilst on patrol I heard voices in a hut. I told my corporal, as there was a curfew on at the time. We entered and there crouched up in a corner was a man and two women. We ejected the man; he was taken to the guardroom and detained. I was left to guard the two women. In the morning we were in for the high jump, the man and two women were brother and sisters. On another occasion we were on a patrol, about midnight the Jews were in the custom of leaving their washing out all night. It was not long before I was sleeping between silk sheets and wearing silk pyjamas.

I was getting on quite well with a young Jewish girl by the name of Tobia Benzwi; her father kept the stores where our company was stationed. Eventually all our troops were dealing there buying goods on credit. When the girl's father found out that I was getting on too well with his daughter, he prevented me from seeing her again and kept her indoors. I retaliated by telling my company commander that he was giving credit and that our troops were paying nearly all their money to him. Straight away the store was put out of bounds. The shopkeeper did everything in his power to get on the right side of me. I would not put up with him though I still carried on meeting Tobia as usual. In 1947 the United Nations created an independent state for both Israel and Palestine to bring peace to the region but even now there is still no peace in the area.

Chapter XI

FRENCH FOREIGN LEGION

By now I was getting fed up of Palestine and the army so it wasn't long before I was making plans to desert from the army. To go on the run, required two of you as conditions here were bad due to the hot climate, sandstorms, arid ground, navigating and most of all the bloody Arabs. I confided with a pal of mine by the name of Titch Taylor. During the ensuing days we collected Arab clothing, we had already noticed that Arabs on trek walked single file and on passing others no word would be spoken, so we had a good chance of getting along alright. I found out that this country had not lived up to my expectations and this land that was supposedly flowing with milk and honey was in fact flowing with rock and sand. Such places as Rebecca's Well, Solomon's Pool, Mount of Olives and the Gate of Damascus were things as far as I was concerned did not exist. I make no bones about it, during active service as a soldier in Palestine in 1929, I became a deserter. By my own admission, I could not take any more of army life. I was 21 years old, I had had enough and wanted to get back to England but what followed was a rough riding time of high adventure. We decided to desert at night, as it was cooler in the evenings. We dressed as Arabs and we got on our way. We only had a small amount of money but we thought that this was not such an important issue as villages and towns were a big distance apart and we could get our main food from the colonies on route. We knew where the other companies of our regiment were and we decided to give these a wide berth. What we meant to do was to get to some place where there were no British people therefore no one would know much of the movements of the British forces. We travelled mostly at night, for the heat in the daytime was unbearable. We had decided that when we did stop it would be near some Jewish colony or Arab village. We were taking a chance here, let me tell you, in the Jewish colonies we put on civilian clothing. Now this was all right to a point. A Palestine Jew does not get tattooed, only the Arabs. Myself being heavily tattooed needed some explaining. We told the Jews that we were English Jews. At the time I spoke some Palestine Yiddish. When I was asked my name, I said it was Ezra Levy. In each colony the Jews were good to us, likewise the Arabs in their villages. The most amusing thing was when we reached big Arab towns we were not far off some of our troops and always cautious about bumping into any army patrols. At times we have sat outside Arab cafés with Arab men having a puff at the Hookah pipe. This is like a large glass bowl with a long pipe attached, we sat in a half circle and the pipe was passed from one to another. The only thing that we had to watch was drinking their water, we had seen the locals drinking it so we thought no harm would come to us.

In the Jewish places food was better, and I quite like the tea in a glass, sugar, no milk and a slice of lemon, it is an excellent drink. We lived on plenty of fruit, oranges, grapes, dates, also melons, which we filched out of the groves when there was no one around.

There was only one main road at this time so we used most of the byways and camel tracks. It was during a sandstorm that my friend went down with dysentery; this was due to eating unwashed fruit or fruit off the floor, at least when picking fruit from the tree you knew it was safe. We had to lie low for at least a fortnight, but with the help of Arabs my friend Titch pulled through. The Arabs fixed us up with a camel train that was heading to Jaffa, so we took the offer and went on our way. The camels were laden with oranges and after a three-day trek we arrived in Jaffa. Our desertion was getting us nowhere, there was no aim to it, just two young men getting sicker and of course getting deeper into trouble. Titch and I decided to go our separate ways and we tried to live off the hot desert land. I roamed the wastes of north Africa for six months, getting what I could in the way of food from the numerous Arab villages. For six months I just mucked in with the Arabs by pretending to be a British Jew. They gave me bread, wild grapes and oranges, and this was my staple diet on the run.

I started to question my motive, what am I achieving? Being this close to British troops I decided to move east towards Jordan. No British troops there I thought. There were some goat herders and they pointed to a town in the distance. They chanted, 'Madaba, Madaba.' That was the name of the village just the other side of the border. As I got closer towards the desert village, a cloud of dust began to get closer and closer and the moment had arrived which was to lead to my *'remarkable experience number one.'* A group of about a dozen Bedouin tribesmen, themselves on camels, spotted me. They rode up to me, a couple of them took me by the arms, and Harry Southall-Owen was theirs! Apparently, in those troubled times, Arab ruffians could make quite a bit of cash on the side for any stray able-bodied man they could find. And they knew exactly where they could take me and make a fast sale.

Naturally, I had no idea what they were going to do with me. They took me to a café, and after about two hours, a party of civilians came in and it was clear that I was to be handed over to them. I thought it must be British Military Police who had come to fetch me back. But the plain clothes men were not British Army chaps at all. They turned out to be officers from the French Foreign Legion, and for twenty Palestinian pounds, Harry was sold there and then by his Arab kidnappers to the Legion. Having deserted anyway, I had little choice but to go quietly, and soon decided that if the Legion had got me, I would stay for two years and then claim French citizenship, thus burying my military identity. But where the future was concerned, the Foreign Legion had it all wrapped up for me in advance. I was drafted into a Foreign Legion regiment of one hundred and eighteen of the worlds roughs and toughs, given a uniform and a rifle, and told to get on with it or else.

The French Foreign Legion was formed in 1831. The main theme running through the Legion was discipline. Right from the time I was bundled in, I was made to realise that I could not answer back I had to do everything I was told. Very soon, the deserter was to begin to pay for his folly. For the first week or two, my duties had to be done at the double, running for supplies, running to peel potatoes, running to clean my rifle, running in the hot sun above the desert base. The routine I was to get used to generally involved five or six weeks fort duty, and then a return to main base. The idea was to march, fully loaded and heavily armed, to fort. There, the Legionnaire was bound to a rota of foot patrols, and guard duty. Many were the times of an attack. Bedouins and Moors who descend from North Africa were persistent snipers and gun fights were the order of the day most of the time. I learned to ride a camel, but it is far harder than it looks. The camel sways from side to side, often at a fair trot. I experienced camel sickness, rather like the feeling of travel sickness, but even worse in a hot climate. In no time at all I was a fully-fledged Legionnaire fighting for France.

There was comradeship among the lads. However, you could not say a word out of place and there was always the chance of being robbed by your own bunk mate. One or two got beaten up in the night. My mates came from all parts; there were Germans, Poles, Swedes, Turks. The international language between us was football. The odd Legionnaire could speak a few languages. They made us sing the Legionnaire song 'Marche de la Legion Etrangere,' every time we marched. One of them, I remember, had a pet dog a scruffy little mongrel. One night, on fort duty, the animal was chained outside. Wild desert dogs attacked in darkness, and all that was left of Rex next morning was the chain and some fur. So, this was desert life in the Legion, the knife edge all the time. To this day as a curt reminder of all this I still have trouble with my feet, so badly did they become blistered through marching across miles of hot sand, but all the marching had a purpose, to track down the enemy. One afternoon I witnessed another torture. My unit had captured a marauding Bedouin, and the sure-fire method of gleaning information began before my eyes. The Bedouin was hung upside down, and his bare soles struck repeatedly with a stout stick. It was the only torture the natives could not stand. It was torture enough though to be a Legionnaire. We rose each bitterly cold morning at 4.30am ready for action. Food was poor, and for me the meat was indigestible. Water was of course scarce, and it was more agonising on route-marching to know the cask at your belt was full of water, but that you cannot drink without permission, water was to be drank only in dire emergency and when ordered. Every other week Legionnaire troops were moved to Morocco where the French were helping the Spanish fight against the Berber tribesmen in a battle they called 'The Rif War.' And so, it went on. After a few months I built my strength back up and defected. On the run again, I travelled to Palestine straight to the British Consulate who handed me over to the Military Police. Titch had been caught six months earlier after the army paid for information to some local Bedouin and they passed on information about two westerners he got apprehended after we parted our ways. The following day at nine o'clock I got cleaned and spruced up and met the consul, he opened the door, I followed him into an office and there was Corporal Lane and two privates, yes, my escort back to my battalion. It took the corporal ages to establish that I was in fact Private Owen. The sun had done its work all right, I was deeply tanned; very thin from malnutrition the only thing that I was recognised by was my initial tattooed on my left wrist even then you only could see it at close examination. Eventually I was escorted back to my company, who during our absence they had moved to another part of Palestine. I was placed in close arrest, transferred to HQ Company and given a Field General Court Martial *FGCM*. This was only awarded when one is on active service, which we were on in Palestine.

I had already made up my mind that I was going to have my ticket, *'kicked out'* so when a list of officer's names was presented to represent me in court I turned them down. Even if I had any chance to soldier on what could an officer do or say in your defence against a hard prosecutor. My motto was try and defend yourself always. While I was waiting for my trial I was looked after quite well and did not want for anything. The talk that was going around that I would be getting my ticket *'finished with the army.'* On the day of my trial the courtroom was set in a large building. The President of the court, I believe, had come from the other end of Suez, Egypt. I had never seen so many *'brass'* officers in my life. My trial lasted just six hours and in defending myself I lay full stress on brutalities and how one's freedom and speech was affected in what had been my problem during my time in the forces. Although I had volunteered for the army I did not think that one could be tied down like this. After my trial I waited for three days for the verdict of the court martial. I had been found guilty of desertion whilst on active service. I was sentenced to imprisonment in the citadel in Cairo, Egypt. Under the command of *BTE* British Troops in Egypt, Cairo Brigade. The King of Egypt at the time was King Ahmed Fuad, the father of King Farouk. In this prison the food was different from what I had been used to, meat red in colour seemed half cooked. mosquitoes and flies were in plenty but we were allowed mosquito nets. One of the worst jobs, whilst here for the first month, was scrubbing different parts of the square under the blazing sun. After a couple of days, I saw Titch in the yard. He had been in there a few weeks prior to me and had been given a longer sentence as his duty officer let him down in the trial. I think defending myself paid off in the long run. A friend of ours Sinbad was brought in. He had been given detention. He knew that we had been given our ticket and were discharged from the army with Ignominy *'kicked out,'* so thinking he could get the same he told the army authorities that he had aided our escape. He was tried, got twenty-eight days detention and had to soldier on.

One day without warning we had been told to pack our kit. *'Remarkable experience number two.'* We were taken to Port Said where there was a liner, the 25,000 tonne Moldavia. By now we knew that we were going home to Blighty, but surely not on this liner? Oh yes, we were! The only clothes we had were the clothes that we were standing up in, just one suit of khaki drill and nothing else. We were treated like VIP's but of course we were. We were taken to the captain's cabin where both he and the purser spoke to us. They told us that only they and no one else knew where we had come from so would we be good enough not to tell any of the crew or passengers of our stay in prison? Would we have our meals with the stewards on the second sitting for meals? There were two classes on this ship first and second class. We could have the same facilities as the passengers. They were just finishing an around the world trip. For the next fortnight we had the time of our life. Oh, what a change to a troopship. I think that the passengers must have guessed something was in the wind because although we could go to their dances we looked rather different in our khaki drill outfit and they with their evening dress. The day approached for us to come to our journeys end, Tilbury was the place for us to disembark. As we got nearer to Tilbury, there we could see the green fields of England; what a beautiful sight. It had been two long years, 'what had I been thinking when I walked across the desert?' As we got closer we could see the military police waiting for us. We were asked to disembark first. The red caps met us and as we entered the customs shed we cast a final glance at the liner and passengers who waved to us and cheered, did they know that we had been in prison in Egypt? I bet they did. We walked straight past the customs officers with our escorts. It must have been hilarious to passers-by as we dressed in khaki drill and tanned on a not so warm a day in England. People must have known we had just come from the Middle East or there about but by now my friend and I were used to being watched and stared at. We were only about half an hour at the barracks getting our civilian gear and what gear it was. The suit was thrown at me, it *'literally'* would have fit a fellow over six feet tall, I am only five feet eight inches tall. The trousers I had to turn up three or four times and the jacket was twice the size. I had a cap with a button in. I had a railway warrant and an escort to the station. I did not get the Kings Shilling, this is where the army tripped up. I have heard of soldiers being drummed out of the army, but never without the Kings shilling. My warrant was made out to Bilston but in this situation, I thought I would get off at the station one before. So, I got off at Ettingshall Road, in the hope that there would not be many people about. It was a Saturday morning so most people would be dressed in their best clobber and I didn't want anybody to see me in these clothes. By various short cuts I neared home, at the top of my street I saw two of my younger sisters talking to two chaps, at the side of them was my mother's dog. My pride would not let me call to my sisters, the dog spotted me and I called him. He came over and I heard one of my sister's say,

"Look at that scruffy chap stroking our dog."

I took no notice and carried on my way home. No one was at home, but I knew where I could find my mother and father, in the Great Western pub. The time would be half past eight, by ten o'clock I had downed about eight pints, I was very drunk after not touching alcohol for months, everyone wanted to hear about my exploits abroad. The punters had a collection for me, it amounted to about forty shillings, good money in those days.

* * * * * * * *

I returned to England at the time of the Great Depression or the Great Slump what we poor folk called it. World Trade fell by half between 1929-1932. Unemployment was 3.5 million and the population at the time was forty-five million. So even though I was glad to get out of the Army I was back home with people who had no work, food was scarce, and the working class lived in abject poverty. There was no work for me and it soon came clear that no work equalled no money which meant no food. I called at every factory in the area and eventually I got a job in a local tube factory doing three jobs for twenty-five shillings per week.

Things gradually began to go well and at the time I had my eye on a pretty waitress called Lilian that worked at the local hotel called the Pipe Hall, near where I lived. I can see her now after all those years, dark with long black curly hair. She wanted nothing to do with me at the time as she thought I was a ne'r-do-well. We eventually started courting and when my mother heard that we were going to get married she turned me out as she didn't approve. I got a room in a public house that had been condemned, it had been turned into living accommodation and its rooms were turned into bedsits. I had a room for five shillings per week, no furniture, no bed, no clothes, just bare boards to lie on. Behind the fireplace were loads of crickets. These insects reminded me of miniature locusts, which I encountered in Palestine. The sound is caused by the rubbing of their back legs, a hideous noise but still it was a shelter over my head. I put up with this for two months and during this time my wife helped me get furniture on the weekly from Hackney Furnishing Limited. This we had for the large sum of six shillings per week. Even though we were living in poverty we were quite happy. Eventually children began to arrive and I had to get a side-line. Always being fond of horses I thought that this would be up my street if I went rag and bone collecting. I hired a horse for ten shillings per week. I kept him in a room the other end of the kitchen that we called the *'brew house'* where one did the washing of clothes. My main concern was to get as many woollens, rags and iron as I could. I managed to clear a profit and with my unemployment pay I could provide a little extra. After a while I got tipped off that someone was going to shop me so I had to pack this in. Times were very bad and some of our dinners were made up of scratching stew, made from one pound of potatoes halfpenny onion, quarter of scratchings, the whole cost about four pennies. Labour pay was the man got eighteen shillings, wife seven shillings, and each child one shilling. Eventually we could not afford to pay for our furniture and it had to be taken off us. Before this happened, I got in touch with the police to see if the bailiff was empowered to this including the bed. I was assured that he could but the bailiff was kind hearted he said, he would get our bed back for us. He kept his promise and at about eight o'clock he arrived with an old bedstead and mattress, we were so glad of this. To make up for extra money I began to help a local coal merchant. He sold coal on provident cheques. In these days people could have clothes and coal on the cheque system, say you had a cheque for three pounds, you could have so much coal delivered for three shillings per week say ten bags for so much, or you could have twenty bags for the large amount of seven shillings and six pence per week. I went to the colliery, loaded up ninety bags of coal with the owner then we would take these to different places; the owner would carry the first bag off the lorry. He would then talk to the woman of the house while I would carry off the other nine or nineteen bags. Now, I was signing on the labour, I knew I was taking a big risk for I could have been prosecuted for fraud. As time went on work in the local factories was getting worse and the queues were getting bigger at the labour exchange. It was that bad that police had to be on duty to control the unemployed. In Bilston where I lived, our population was around thirty thousand and of these about five thousand were out of work.

Chapter XII

UNEMPLOYMENT SECRETARY

A movement was formed called the Unemployed Workers Movement and I became the secretary of the Bilston branch. The government had created a scheme whereby if one had been drawing unemployment benefit for a duration one had to go and do a week's work on what we called the Poverty Bank. This was land levelling of slag heaps with pick and shovel for two shillings per week on top of your labour pay. It was meant to be a model scheme to train the unemployed; it was cheap labour, to level the ground in Loxdale, Bilston. We set out to fight this so-called 'train the unemployed.' Men were called on to do this work, yes men that did not know what a square meal was. They looked as if they were ready for the grave, never mind doing work. Now a certain newspaper was in circulation, 'The Daily Worker'. It was founded in 1930. Some people said it was receiving funds from Moscow. At the time Stalin was on the side of Hitler. It all changed when the Germans declared war on the Soviet Union, the paper became a strong supporter of the British War effort. We sold the paper and people who were not in the *NUWM,* sold it as well. The pennies taken by selling this newspaper were only being sent to Russia. This paper may have been a blind for the Communist Party but there were no communists in our branch. My great friend now was one by the name of Benjamin Bilboe, *Ben Bilboe,* he was the leader of the National Unemployment Workers Movement in the 1930's and later became the Mayor of Bilston. He also had seen active service in the Great War even though he lied about his age, he was too young to enlist. He went to St Martins School in Bradley, Bilston. He was a self-educated fellow, half of my town loved him and the other half hated him…*Tories.* He was our leader and we, the unemployed, looked to him for guidance. He was a great speaker and he knew what he was talking about. We held classes and every one of our committee knew what role he would have to play if called upon.

Chapter XIII

BATTLES WITH THE MOSLEYITES

The old age pensioners were getting a rough deal so we used to collect food, coal and wood, from the rich to keep those poor souls. The police even kept a close eye on us, for by now they thought that we were Bolsheviks. They did nothing to antagonise the new movement that had started up.

The Fascist Party, Oswald Mosley's party, was becoming a popular movement in the mid to late 1930's due to the far right emerging under the influence of Adolf Hitler in Germany. Oswald was a well to do sort of character his party were more commonly known as the British Union of Fascists, *BUF*. At his meetings Oswald Mosley's Black Shirts were always represented by ex-boxers and roughens, heckling and at his meetings protesters were dealt with in a rough way and thrown out of the conference. It was the unemployed that was treated with contempt and the police seemed to sympathise with the fascists. Something had got to be done by parliament for the unemployed. A hunger march began from Scotland with the biggest contingent being from Jarrow. At different stages of the hunger march more people formed up and by the time it reached Wolverhampton, it was thousands strong. Hot soup and tea was provided at different places and each night they bedded down in different halls. Many well-known labour leaders had much to do in the way of helping and marching on to the houses of parliament. Among them being Ernest Bevin, Miss Helen Wilkinson, Miss Maggie Bondfield and the communist Professors Haldame and Megoven.

At the House of Commons so many hunger marchers were admitted and leaflets were showered on the floor of the house. At one of our meetings on the Poverty Bank, Ben Bilboe was arrested, charged under the rioting act and sent to prison. We had already got an election campaign set in motion, for Bilboe was standing for election as councillor in the new town ward. The big Tory Industrialist J Toole had held this seat for years. While Ben Bilboe was in jail the elections were held and Bilboe was elected as councillor, this was a turn up for the books. This was to be a turning point for the town as it had been ruled by the Tories for many years. Now two Labour councillors represented them. I never sought election as a councillor myself but I was the instigator arranging meetings for potential candidates. In one of the council elections we had as many as six candidates. I was never a communist but on occasions I did allow communists to hold meetings at my one roomed house, Dr Bradshaw, Tom Roberts and Tom Sykes. Sykes was later killed in the Spanish Civil War. We were that bad off that they used to send for biscuits and give us money to get tea, sugar and milk.

The *NUWM*, had now began functioning all over the country. We rented a room behind a watch repairer but found out the proprietor was spying on us for the police, so we packed this place up and we were made welcome at one of the churches. We had the use of one of the rooms but we still had trouble from the police. One day, on the footpath opposite the labour exchange in front of private houses, my friend and I posted two notices on trees. The manager of the exchange sent for the police. We were taken to the police station where I explained to the superintendent of police that the two trees were not on Ministry of Labour property, he allowed us to go. I remember being sent for a job at the new works which had sprung up alongside a poverty bank. Here I was employed at six pence per hour. I had to take this job or lose my unemployment benefit. Of course, one could put in as many hours as possible, for instance seventy hours would bring in about thirty-five shillings per week. Even so you could always pay a trip to the pawnshop. I could not afford a best suit, as times were very hard, you could get five shillings loaned on your wife's wedding ring, not knowing when you could redeem it. I never had any shame in going into a pawnshop, everybody was doing the same. The country was in a dire situation.

Due to my activities in the *NUWM*, I did not reign long at my job, as I used to sell the Daily Worker in the factory where I worked. The management had no alternative but give me the sack. Their sacking of me made little difference to me for it entitled me to claim unemployment benefit. If I had left on my own accord I would have had to wait six weeks before I could have got any benefit.

We could foresee that trouble was brewing in Spain. This was where the Italian Air Force came into its own as they fought on the side of Franco against King Alphonso. The International Brigade sprang up in different European countries including England. They were soldiers who fought for the royalists of Spain against fascism. Three names that were prominent now were Franco who remained neutral in the 1939-1945 war, Mussolini and Hitler. The Italian dictator invaded defenceless Abyssinia, now Ethiopia, and two years later Hitler began his invasion of Austria, Czechoslovakia, Hungary and Poland. A fourth one also in the limelight was Oswald Mosley. There was also an Irishman by the name of William Joyce, known later as Lord Haw Haw. When he found out that he could not oust Mosley as leader, he went to Germany, as he was more of a Nazi than a fascist. This man used to broadcast from Germany during the Second World War. At first, we used to laugh at him but later the British listened into his sinister broadcasts on the bombing of Britain.

I was still trying by various ways and means to get extra money for my wife and family by doing different jobs and at the same time drawing my unemployment pay. It was a big risk but still quite a few were on the fiddle. Saturday nights I spent selling fruit and flowers outside one of the shops in the main street of Bilston finishing about eleven in the evening for this I received five shillings and a box of bruised fruit. Eventually I obtained employment at Sankey's Bankfield, a large steel company working on power shears. Wages were around four pounds per week plus bonus. I was never allowed to get above twenty-five shillings per week bonus, but still it was a decent job. One woman worked on the front of the shears with myself and two girls on the back. It was here that one of the classes that I had been condemning on my political spheres became a friend to me, he was Mr Charles Sankey. In these days one was not allowed to have lunch whilst working, or smoke unless you sneaked off to the toilets. Everyone ate their lunch on the sly at about eleven am, Mr Sankey would appear, he knew quite well employees would snack whilst working. I had not been there long when I was having my lunch, eating while I was working, Mr Sankey came up to me and asked what was the reason I was eating. I had my answer, I said,

"This machine I have to oil each morning at eleven o'clock so I need to stand by it, if I didn't it would break down."

He said, "A fair excuse, carry on."

Our dismal, harsh domestic situation was improving slightly now I could afford to have a new suit for one shilling per week. I still carried on with my NUWM activities while I was working.

I was still lobbying the chief sanitary inspector for a council house, as the crickets were just about getting on my nerves. I was meeting with no success until one day I had an idea. I got a large envelope marked on it On His Majesty's Service *O.H.M.S* and addressed it to the Minister of Health, Houses of Parliament, London. I put about a dozen crickets in this envelope sealed it up and my way up to the sanitary inspector's department. I told the sanitary inspector a Mr Fred Barnet of my intentions, he said,

"You would not do that would you,"

for I was also going to send a covering letter to Miss Margaret Bondfield who was a leading British Labour politician and the first female Cabinet minister, telling her the conditions under which we were living. He gave me the keys to a house to move into the next day. Overjoyed I got my furniture loaded onto a horse and wagon and I was waiting outside the house at nine o'clock the next morning, *Saturday*. The people occupying the house had not moved out so we had to wait and moved in about one o'clock.

Now and again Mr Charles Sankey used to come talking to me and many was the time that he used to give me parcels of his cast-off clothes. One day after giving me some clothes, he said,

"Harry, you don't look pleased," I said, "No sir, you have just insulted me by giving me a Billy Cook," *hardhat*, he just laughed.

He was a good man I remember him getting plaques made of the fallen from the Great War and mounting them at the works as a reminder of the ultimate sacrifice. One of the most touching times that one remembers was when King Edward the Eighth, announced his abdication over the radio, I know there were a lot of tears shed that night, for he was liked and respected by the working class. It was now the 10th December 1936. The Prime Minister was Stanley Baldwin who retired in 1937 vilified for the high unemployment of the 1930's and was succeeded by Neville Chamberlain who said, 'Hitler would not invade Poland.' I tried to start a union at Sankey's works but was unsuccessful, no one was interested, the world was changing and Germany was making its mark.

Chapter XIV

RE-JOINING THE ARMY

There was a lot of talk about war and one knew that it would not be long before we were at war with Germany once again. I came to leave my place of employment under very amusing circumstances. The local factories were busy filling sandbags in preparation for war. The council were offering employment at filling sandbags at one penny per hour. My firm said that we had to fill these sandbags at one shilling per hour. About two dozen of us downed tools and we went black out painting at another factory. This entailed painting all windows and glass roofs with black paint so that the light from inside the factory would not show outside, this was a precaution for air raids. We declared war on Germany, September 3rd, 1939. I thought it would be a dereliction of my duty if I did not sign up for King and country especially with my previous army experience. I was now 31 years old.

I volunteered and was signed in at Wolverhampton. This time I was going to make sure that I would do good for after all these years I was just about fed up with Fascists and Nazism. I remember going to the local picture house to watch the latest news and Hitler was advancing rapidly through Europe. The equipment that the Germans had, seemed advanced and they had much of it. In the Great Depression we did nothing to bolster our armies, the Germans on the other hand used it to their advantage and built a war machine strong enough to conquer Europe. They well and truly caught us off guard. Even though a few politicians including Winston Churchill, warned the government of Germanys military power and imminent onslaught, the Prime Minister, Neville Chamberlain and a few other ministers turned a blind eye to it, believing Hitler would stick to his word. He was only interested in the Sudetenland, the area between Czechoslovakia and Germany. He was in fact after the whole of Europe, maybe the world. Once Hitler invaded Poland we had no choice to declare war on Germany on the 3rd September 1939. We had some catching up to do, Hitler's war machine was on the move, ours were barely off the ground.

When I was sworn in on Friday 6th October 1939 for services in World War Two, I told my wife that I had been called up due to my previous army experience when in fact I volunteered but I didn't tell her that until after the war. I was sent to Cardiff to join other men, there were even six convicts from different jails who had volunteered to serve their country, they were the finest mates you could ever meet. I had to report to the Welsh Regiment at Cardiff, hand in my papers and await orders of where I had to go. The volunteering age was 18 to 42. Let me start here, of my first encounter with *'ticket of leave men.'* It was a document issued for parole, convicts who could be trusted released early and with a war they signed up. These were volunteers from different prisons who were making up of the first contingent of the *'BEF'* British Expeditionary Force for France.

One old chap that was with me for three years had not been to prison, but I knew for a fact that he was sixty-seven years old. He had fought in three wars, The Boer War 1899, Boxer Rebellion 1901, and the 1914 -1918 War. This was his fourth War. He had his medal ribbons on his civvy jacket, among these was the South African ribbon. The sergeant of the guards saw this and said,

"If you are only 42, what are you doing with this ribbon?"

The old sweat replied, "I've told you, I'm 42."

Hence the name we gave him 'Pop Dyson.' He came from Oldham, Lancashire.

I must state that when I got attested at Wolverhampton, I gave my proper name, former regiment, number (4910683) and service. After being fitted out with our khaki and equipment, we headed for Southampton. This is all we were sent to France with, one battle dress suit, one steel Brodie helmet, one respirator; we had no arms or ammunition. This was our dress for the first six months of our service. Our first place of stay was Plouray in Brittany and our shelter was an old cowshed which had no door and just a canvas frontage. Bed was a paillasse filled with straw and homemade bed boards which sat four inches off the ground. Winter had just started and under these conditions we had to soldier the worst winter France had in the last seventy years. Our job was to build ammunition dumps and unload ammunition that was being sent over from England, (.303 bullets and shells). Our Regiment was the Royal Army Ordnance Corps (RAOC) and my job role was as part of a chain-handling shells which was a chain of about twenty soldiers passing shells to each other and stacking them underground in fields, caching the ammunition for later in the war, it was back breaking stuff. We worked about ten or twelve hours per day, a break of ten minutes each morning and afternoon and half an hour break for dinner. Hot dinner was served in our mess tins which were cleaned out after with cold water and wiped with grass. On returning to our billets they were lit by candles and there was a fire to warm us.

Chapter XV

PROMOTION

Our youngest soldier with us was just seventeen, and our oldest was 'Pop Dyson.' One day our company commander Major Proctor called me into the office and asked me if I would like to take my first stripe, *Lance Corporal*, which I took and within two months I was made up to a Sergeant. I was one of the senior sergeants in the British Expeditionary Force and in November 1940 we had our name changed to the Royal Pioneer Corps. The cap badge was a pick and shovel. It was a combatant corps. One of my men a *'proper case'* went by the name of 'Jock Wilson,' and his previous regiment was The Seaforth Highlanders who were associated with the northern highlands of Scotland. He used to be a 'knight of the road' and a proper villain in his own right. One day he said to me, "Sarge, can you make me the billet orderly? I will get some logs sawn and get a fire going for when the lads come up from the dumps." I knew he was a bit of a card, but I gave him the job, little knowing what I was letting myself in for. For the first day or so, everything had gone quite well, a fire awaiting us when we got in at night to dry our battle-dress. We came back one day to no fire and old Jock was blind drunk, bottles strewn across the billet, where he had got his wine from we did not know, until the old madam from the café came to see me. The wall of our cow shed at the end, was the same wall that divided a café cellar from our billet. He had removed the wooden boards and climbed through into her place, got wine and other bottles of different spirits, crawled back and replacing the boards after him hoping he wouldn't have been caught and could do a return visit. She was adamant she was going to the company commander. We collected what money we had on the promise Jock would repay us, deep down I knew he would be a good soldier and I needed all the experienced men I could muster.

From here I was sent on a passive air defence course. This was training on how to use anti-aircraft machine guns and barrage balloons. I was away for one month and then we had to prepare for moving to Brest which was located on the north-western tip of France, to work on the docks unloading ships. For about two or three months after arriving at Brest, I had to instruct troops in gas drill, having passed my test *1st class*. Working at the docks we were under the control of the Royal Engineers. Our job was to unload train rails, goods, foodstuffs and general stores off the boats. We worked roughly twelve hours per day. Our company was now about three hundred strong and we worked in two shifts around the clock. Our men were split to work in different holds of the ships. The old timers always used to try and get in the holds that contained the stores, whisky, tin beer, chocolate and cigarettes.

I have marched my men back to their billets many a time half-drunk and leaning onto each other. My former service stood me in good stead for having to instil discipline into these men. So far, the only fighting that we had seen was between our own boys after they had been drinking amongst themselves.

We had always been told by the French people that they could be the Germans, hadn't we got the Maginot line fully manned?

The Maginot line named after the French Minister of War Andre Maginot, was a line of concrete fortifications, obstacles and weapons installations built by the French to deter invasion by the Germans. It covered the whole of the French and German border a thousand troops lived underground manning artillery guns mounted on retractable turrets it had miles of underground tunnels, kitchens, bars, and wine cellars.

I felt sorry for old 'Pop Dyson,' I got my company commander to give him a stripe '*Lance Corporal*' and put him in charge of sanitary and ablutions. Our toilet comprised of four pieces of wood, six feet high and around these were fixed hessian sacking, a pit dug in the ground and a length of wood fixed two feet above ground. To go to the toilet was a balancing trick. Old Pop was one of the best soldiers that I had ever had the privilege of working with. For our ablutions and baths, he scrounged an old wine vat, built a fire trench that he continuously kept going and scrounged one-gallon square petrol tins that he filled with water with the help of French children. When we arrived back each night hot water was in plenty, all tins having been carried and tipped in the vat, this bathhouse was surrounded by hessian to make it private. At this stage our buckshee rations were fifty cigarettes, one bar of chocolate and one bar of soap. Each week the chocolate was collected and given to the children for their services. We were now settled down into army routine and had take part in parades and drill. Most of my company except for the younger soldiers had previous army service so this of course came in their stride. Our General Officer Commanding of the *BEF* at this phase of the war was Field Marshall John Standish Surtees Pendergast Vereker, 6th Viscount Gort, VC, GCB, CBE, DSO and 2 Bars, MVO, MC nicknamed (Tiger Gort), he was awarded the Victoria Cross in the Great War but he didn't get along with the Secretary of State for War, Hore Belisha MP. It became known as the 'Pillbox Affair' due to them despising one another. Tiger Gort died just after the war in 1946 due to liver cancer. His message around Christmas time 1939 to the mothers of Great Britain was that if any of their sons were under the age of 18 they could have them home for Christmas, none of my boys took the offer. Our next move was to Rennes; here our strength went up to about three hundred other ranks. One commanding officer and two officers and numerous sergeant's and corporal's. We were encamped under canvas at Rennes football stadium and here we had extra equipment issued to us. I had the responsibility for administration of all intakes that were drifting from other areas of France. Regiments were being made up to strength and were being sent up the line, not knowing that in a few weeks we would be retreating to England under pressure from the Germans moving west.

Chapter XVI

CHANGING MY NAME

One day I was sent for by the assistant adjutant. A message had come through from the war records office requesting that in future would I sign Sergeant H Southall-Owen on all quittance rolls and army records and they gave me a new number 7605842. A new life for me had begun. I think that they had found out that Private H Owen, 4910683 who had been discharged from the army with ignominy twelve years previously was the same man who had been promoted to sergeant. They could not really kick me out now, hence the hyphen in my name. One of the biggest surprises was that some of my former pals that I left in Palestine had reported to me in Rennes. They were reserve men that had been called up; they had already been up the line and had come back for a rest. Imagine their surprise when they saw that I had to have their kit off them! How was it, they were saying, that Brasso Owen, my former nickname in the Stafford's was now a sergeant after being kicked out? I passed the information on to them.

"Call me Brasso," I said, "But if there is anyone about spring to attention and say Sarge."

* * * * * * * *

For our tea on a Friday we always had hard biscuits and tinned herrings so one of the sergeants had a brain wave. By taking off the wrapper he could sell them to the French saying they were English chocolates. Each tin weighed 12 ounces; he sold them for two shillings per tin. The same thing happened the next Friday but when we arose on the Saturday morning all the tents were covered with fish. We had a job getting our lines ready for the commanding officers inspection. This was another way of fiddling. It was at this stadium that we met Jimmy Hogan, the famous football coach. He came to train some of our boys and he was coaching in France at the outbreak of the war.

We were passing our time now by full scale training, musketry and arms drill. We were on a proper military footing and we were doing guard duties at vulnerable points. Gone was the unloading of ships and dumps, we were qualified to go up the line. Our next move was Saint Malo, France. Here our job was to guard the docks and railways. My commanding officer had great faith in me as a leader of men so the running of this was down to me. This entailed guards of twenty-four hours duration and I had got to work the roster so that each man had a night in bed after doing his guard. We sported two tier beds by now. Each man had been issued a rifle and ammunition was kept in the guardroom.

One day out of the blue we heard that Hitler gave the order to invade France. It was now May 10th 1940. Hitler ordered one of his best Generals Erwin Rommel to invade France but not through the Maginot Line but through the Ardennes Forest catching the French by surprise. The French government didn't believe the Germans would come through the forest this is what caused the British to retreat back to Dunkirk. A Division of the British Expeditionary Force the 51st Highland Division which were separated from the rest of the BEF and put under the command of the French Army and told to help defend the Maginot Line. They had been in France since January and numbered twenty thousand troops from mainly Scottish regiments. They were told by Churchill to stay and assist the French at all cost. The Germans forced a wedge on the end of Belgium; the Maginot Line proved useless. The French forces were trapped in their own fortress. The 51st Division were now cut off from the rest of the BEF, Winston Churchill told Major General Victor Fortune the commander of the 51st Division to fight to the last man.

Chapter XVII

EVACUATION OF SAINT MALO

We heard about Dunkirk from the French workers on the docks, they have heard it on their radios. The evacuation of Dunkirk happened between the 26th May to the 4th June 1940 and was code named Operation Dynamo. Between the 15th to the 25th June 1940 the evacuation of Saint Malo happened, this was code named Operation Ariel. The Nazis main weapon in France was the fifth column, the French traitors passing on information to the enemy. Churchill had taken over as Prime Minister some two months before this. Tiger Gort had gone so had Hore Belisha. Things were looking bad.

We had been told that 51st Division and the French Army had been involved in heavy fighting and had made their way back to the French coast hoping for an evacuation back to England but running short of ammunition and saving the lives of his men Major General Fortune had no option but to surrender his forces to General Rommel. The division were completely encircled by the 7th Panzer Division. General Fortunes 51st Division played no part in the rest of the war they were held prisoners until 1945. The intelligence we were receiving was that Rommel would be heading further South towards my division but after hearing the news Churchill promised that we would be evacuated.

The prologue describes what we did east of Rennes. Once we arrived back at the football stadium my battalion had already left. There were quite a few stragglers so as the only sergeant around I decided to parade them and start marching to Saint Malo. We received orders to embark on any vessel that was available once we got to the port. I did a head count and began to march away, when I noticed one missing, I halted them, asked where Private Black was, they told me he had gone to get his tea rations. I wasn't impressed there was no time to waste.

Eventually after picking up Private Black we moved off at the double. After a couple of miles, we managed to hitch a lift on another battalion's truck otherwise it's a long forty miles to the port, seeming even longer after last evenings escapade. We were tired, short of equipment and desperate to get home to re-group. Eventually we came along the quayside and got aboard. One boat that came in and out of St Malo loaded and unloaded three or four times in a fortnight was the RMS Lancastria. It was a British Cunard liner requisitioned by the government. It was attacked by the Luftwaffe and there was only an estimate of how many people were lost, in the region of between 3000-6500 people perished. It was packed to the brim to get as many people back to England. It made the disaster the greatest loss of life on a British ship and was kept secret by Winston Churchill. It sank twenty minutes after it was bombed by the Germans, the Luftwaffe then decided to strafe any survivors left in the water, near the French port of Saint-Nazaire on the 17th June 1940 fewer than 2,477 survived.

After dodging the Luftwaffe, the RAF intervened and our boat put us to safety at Southampton. After a good meal, brush up, and haversack rations we were put on a train, destination unknown to us. On looking through the carriage windows passing through stations their nameplates were blacked out. This seemed strange to us, for nothing like this happened in France. Eventually we arrived at Bournemouth. We had a week here before being sent to Monkton Farleigh, Bradford-on-Avon in Wiltshire, about three miles from Bath. Here we were issued with new kit and as well as our personal weapons we were supplied with light machine guns. After full-scale training we had the honour of doing guard duties at Colerne Airfield, Chippenham. I saw here the great Polish airman General Wladyslaw Sikorski, a legend of the skies he was killed in 1943 after his plane crashed after leaving Gibraltar. One part of our company was doing guard duties at Corsham on the edge of the Cotswolds, West Wiltshire. It was my good fortune to be detailed to form a variety concert party and later a dance band was formed. The concert party travelled to all the local villages to perform for troops and civilians alike. There was that many acts in the show that it lasted two hours.

I was taking a new made up sergeant whose job previously was in the orderly room in drilling men, as we marched down the road to get to the parade ground an officer was coming in our direction, I said to the sergeant,

"Now then eyes right, here have a bash," he shouted, "Eyes right," he gave the officer a smart salute and shouted, "Eyes back again," instead of saying, 'Eyes front.' It did one good to have a bit of humour.

Another laugh that I had was with a private who wanted an interview with the commanding officer. He was rather reluctant to tell me what he wanted his interview for. I told the commanding officer and marched the private into the office; he told the commanding officer that he wanted compassionate leave because his wife was having a baby.

"That's nothing to do with me, march him out sergeant," said the Commanding Officer.

In all my soldiering I had never charged a private, the one person that I did charge was a sergeant. He had hopped off with the dance bands fee, he oversaw them that night. It could not have happened at a worse place than in Bathampton, which is two miles East of Bath. Queen Mary had an interest at this village, and the lady in charge or responsible for the dance had his signature on the receipt. Taff was a good soldier and it hurt me a lot when I had to pick him up from the Military Police Headquarters, Cheltenham.

My next job was training air force ground staff to do drill foot and rifle for soon a new regiment was to be formed called the RAF Regiment. I had a hand in training these and eventually when they were formed their uniform was blue with their duties being the same as the military. When they were ready for taking over their duties, we had to concentrate on our own regimental duties. It wasn't long before rumours started to circulate that we were going to be transferred to a foot regiment. We got put into a battalion of the Suffolk Regiment. This meant goodbye to the old pick and shovel cap badge. It was an honour to belong to the Pioneer Corps. We now had to put in plenty of practice down at the firing range and get used to handling hand grenades, spigot mortars and different small weapons. One of these that I got to become an expert with was The Thompson Machine Gun, *'Tommy Gun.'* It was .45 Calibre, weighed 10 pounds and could fire 600 rounds per minute.

One of my renowned officers now was an Irish man by the name of Captain William Howard, 8th Earl of Wicklow more commonly known as Lord Clonmore, scruffy little sod, he could never get dressed properly for a parade but he was always in the thick of everything and you could bet your life on him. He was well respected amongst the ranks. It didn't matter what you looked like if you had good leadership in battle that was the main thing.

Our boys were taking more pride in themselves now and it was noticeable how the sick parade had dwindled down. Moral was good, this was a sign that things were going down quite well. Our battalion was the 30th Battalion Suffolk Regt. Some regiments had a battalion; which comprised young soldiers from the schools like the one that I had in my earlier schooling, they were noticeably fitter than some of the other battalions.

I had orders for an interview with the commanding officer. He had put me forward for an award for what I did against the enemy train but the 'General' turned it down due to my previous army record before the war. I wasn't really bothered but on the other hand he had received inquiries about me from senior officers to see if I wanted to join a new regiment that was being formed. At the time it was nameless and my duties would require me to help in the administration of the regiment. It was through my experience that I had been recommended. I said goodbye to my company and reported Tilshead, Salisbury Plain. It was a tented village, only two brick buildings and that was the ablutions. I still didn't have a clue what I was letting myself in for but I was used to adventure and if it was anything against *Jerry* I was up for it.

As the new joiners started to form up on the drill square we got to know our new regiment. It was going to be called **'The Glider Pilot Regiment.'** The gliders were to be used in the transportation of airborne troops. It was now February 1942.

Chapter XVIII

GLIDER PILOT REGIMENT

On 21st June 1940, Winston Churchill gave the order to form a force of 5,000 parachutists and glider-borne troops. The Glider Pilot Regiment was an elite regiment of the British Army which was formed in December 1941. It wasn't a new idea, many forces around the world had been using gliders to deploy troops. The novelist Barbara Cartland had an interest in gliders. She designed a glider in 1931 to deliver mail. She also completed a two-hundred-mile tow in a two-seater glider and raced an express train from London to Blackpool and won.

Members of the regiment were primarily drawn from volunteers from other parts of the army. Only those who achieved the highest standards were selected for flying training, initially training on powered aircraft before learning to fly gliders. Once fully qualified, they would fly huge unpowered aircraft, capable of carrying troops, jeeps, artillery pieces and even tanks. They would achieve extraordinary feats of flying, landing on unprepared landing zones behind enemy lines, and taking up arms to fight beside the troops which they carried into battle. They adopted whatever role was required of them, operating as pilots, infantry and medics. The General Officer Commanding of the Airborne Division was Lieutenant General Sir Fredrick Arthur Montague 'Boy' Browning, one of the youngest Generals in the British Army at the age of forty-four. He was an Olympic Bobsleigh competitor and the husband of the author Dame Daphne du Maurier. He led Operation Market Garden. Commanding officer of the Paratroopers and a glider pilot was Lieutenant Colonel Rock, age about thirty-one. The commanding officer of the Glider Pilot Regiment was Lieutenant Colonel Chatterton age about thirty-two. He decided that the Glider Pilot Regiment should produce men who were every bit as proficient in fighting on the ground as they were at flying in the air, and to this end he employed drill sergeants from the Brigade of Guards to oversee a thoroughly punishing training regime that would weed out all but the very best men. Chatterton's speech to the Regiment in 1942 rather summed up his approach:

"We will forge this regiment as a weapon of attack... Not only will we be trained as pilots, but in all we do... I shall be quite ruthless... Only the best will be tolerated. If you do not like it, you can go back whence you came."

So, you see these were surely the youngest leaders of one division. Age of the glider pilots when they had passed all their tests was between eighteen to thirty-two years of age. I was marched into the office of the Commanding Officer, Lt Col Chatterton. He had been reading my army record and was very impressed including the bit where I absconded in Palestine and how I managed to make my way around the region without being apprehended by the Military Police. He was quite interested in what I had got up to in the French Foreign Legion and what training we did. We chatted about when he got evacuated from Dunkirk and myself from Saint Malo. He was a strict disciplinarian and only wanted the best men for the regiment. Most of the entrants that we had had spent a large amount of their service in company offices and orderly rooms. They had to have knowledge of Morse Code and a smattering of foreign languages, be in good shape, super fit and they were in for some intensive training. Among these were sons of doctors, clergy, teachers. Most were students and all were very well educated although some may never have seen a rifle or done any spit and polishing in their soldiering until they came to the Glider Pilot Regiment. These men were to get their wings and they knew they had to work hard for them. I trained the men on the Bren gun and Tommy gun, every morning we would do a five-mile run broken down in five minutes run, five minutes' walk in full battle dress if I thought they didn't put enough effort on the run we would go around again finishing off doing ten miles. These future glider pilots needed to be trained to a very high soldiering standard because as soon as they had landed the glider or in some cases crash landed the glider they would be part of the ground force. On their initial interviews they were told they would be flying into enemy held territory and what could be a 'one-way ticket.' I can honestly say that after six weeks of square bashing, route marches, cross-country running with battle order on, bulling up, educational work, these men were as good as any guards, including their drill. In fact, they were better. It took exceptional courage to fly a glider with no engine, being shot at. On many occasion I was in the back of the gliders flying at two thousand feet with just the sound of the wind and in the winter, it was bitterly cold. Sometimes I would travel in the back of a glider with loads of sandbags providing ballast which sometimes would slide all over the place with the pilots struggling with the controls and me in the back trying to re-adjust them, but I would receive extra pay for this and good training for the pilots.

After their period of training had finished each squad went down to RAF camps such as Kidlington or High Wycombe. Here they did training in planes with so many hours dual control then so many hours solo. After passing out on these they went onto glider training. When a squadron had passed this course, they came back to Tilshead and were presented with their wings. These were The Glider Pilot Wings. The usual custom for this was they were paraded on a Friday morning and inspected by Lt General Browning. It fell as a great honour to me, on one or two occasions to be present on parade during the presentations of wings to the pilots. I would hand a pin and wing to the general who would then pin it to the left breast of the pilot. The General would go out of his way to speak to anyone in his division, for let it be known that he commanded the finest division in the British Army. Immediately after this they all went on fourteen days leave promoted to Staff Sergeant. It came as a big blow when we lost the Commanding Officer, Lieutenant Colonel Rock when he lost his life in a Hotspur Glider during a night flight over Shrewton, Wiltshire, on the 27th September 1942, he died two weeks later, on the 8th October 1942, at Tidworth Hospital. There were quite a few accidents in the early days. I also help train the pilots who were involved in a sabotage attack in Norway code named Operation Freshman, on a heavy water plant but due to severe weather the gliders didn't reach the objective meaning some of the pilots and Royal Engineer sappers were captured and executed by the Gestapo.

Eventually our admin staff had grown to about two hundred sergeants and other ranks and the 1st Battalion Gliders to about six hundred sergeants. Now, I was good pals with the Sergeants mess caterer. Our cooks were from the Army Catering Corps. Our waiter from our own admin staff and the President was the Regimental Sergeant Major from the Irish Guards. He had a responsibility with other Sergeant Majors for drilling the pilots. He had a good job here, for as you know, everything now in the way of foodstuffs and confectionery, soap, sweets, biscuits and cigs were on rations. He would get me white ink which he bought from Devizes in Wiltshire. I sold it to the other sergeants it was used for whitening their stripes, the price I believe at the time was one shilling a bottle. Our admin contained one or two characters and one of the occasions that two of them were waiting for a lift into Devizes from the village was when a dispatch driver came around the corner he signalled to these two that it was possible to get a lift, as there was a car coming along behind him. They signalled the driver and the car stopped. Inside was a lady, the driver told them to get in. One sat by the lady and the other sat by the driver. They proceeded on and during the conversation the lady said she was the Queen Mother 'Queen Mary.' One of them said,

"If you be Queen Mary I be Winston Churchill."

On arriving at Devizes, she gave them a medallion with her initials on. This was reported in the evening newspaper.

By now the Air Force Division was at full strength comprising of glider pilots, admin staff, paratroopers and airborne troops. One battalion of these was 2nd Battalion the South Staffordshire Regiment, my former Regiment in Palestine. They would be trained for an assault on Ponte Grande Bridge using what we were called Horsa Gliders as these could carry nearly thirty troops. In the build-up training which lasted a few weeks we lost thirteen men from crashes. Things were all a bustle now and it was the practice that each Wednesday afternoon we attended a lecture given by scientists or professors. The training was intense and diverse, different from the normal army regiment training.

Chapter XIX

RETURNED TO UNIT

Since my being in the service 1939 it was now 1942 my wife had become in arrears with her rent and was half way through a difficult pregnancy. Through the war we would get the occasional rest and recuperation, R&R and if we were in England this would be an opportunity to get home but just for a few days. Unknowingly to me my Commanding Officer Lieutenant Colonel Chatterton, the Padre and my town clerk in Bilston had decided for the money to be stopped out of my pay, that was against all rules for I should have been consulted. I knew nothing at all about this so of course in an interview I went off at the deep end. The same afternoon we had a lecture, I believe that afternoon the lecturer was a Professor Low. In his speeches he would discuss Russia. I remember seeing him a year before in 1941 giving a lecture and at the time he said that Russia would on the side of the Nazis. This rather stung me and when question time came I said that I thought that if Russia did come into the war she would be on the side of the Allies, he laughed and thought it was utter nonsense. A few months later she entered the war under Operation Barbarossa now on the side of the Allies, he recognised me I also reminded him of that day, he was rather sheepish. Two days later I was told to see the company clerk, I received a rail warrant to my home town to sort out the arrears and have a week off part of my R&R!

Arriving home my wife was rather upset apart from the arrears she told me that one of the Air Raid Precaution Wardens, *'ARPs'* had reported her to the police due to leaving a gap between the curtains letting light shine through during an air raid. The next day she was ordered to the police station and given a fine. The jumped up little Hitler *'Warden'* could have knocked the front door and asked her to close the curtains. He knew me being from such a small town but for some of the home guard they were quite jealous of us fellows on the front line and felt were more important. I hastily went and paid him a visit. I explained he was out of order, treating my wife like that as she was looking after a young family and pregnant while her husband was away fighting *'Jerry.'* I can now say that once I had finished with him no complaints were ever made again. So, I thought. The police called my commanding officer and told them that a sergeant from the Glider Pilot Regiment had assaulted a warden. On returning to Tilshead I got a request to report back to my former regiment the Suffolk Regiment on a request that the regiment were deploying on operations and were short of senior non-commissioned officers.

* * * * * * * * * *

The main cities and towns were now being heavily bombed by *'Jerry'* and one of the main targets was West Ham, which I believe was the biggest borough in England at the time. I had been drafted down there and our main job was guarding warehouses and other buildings that had been bombed. In this squad was myself, a Lieutenant and forty-two men. Here I was left in charge, for my Lieutenant liked the bottle and was not available only to pay the men out. It was my responsibility to see that the rota system was running properly, in these days a soldier had to have at least a night in bed after doing twenty-four hours guard and it was very hard to get the quota of weekend passes which these men were entitled to. As time went on they were getting uneasy, some lived locally and were married. Of course, when I told the Lieutenant, I knew that I had made an enemy of him. I was waiting for him to come in one night in our office when the phone rang, it was a phonogram from Bilston Police Station saying my wife was very ill in child birth and I should get home. This was compassionate leave, which I should have. My officer came in half drunk as usual, I told him and if he wanted confirmation he must ring Bilston police station.

He refused to do so. I rang up my Head Quarters at Ingatestone, Essex. I was told to proceed on leave. I told my officer, he was livid and refused to give me a warrant or pass.

I was ten shillings short of my fare so I borrowed it off one of the men and I went on leave, got home in time for my wife to give birth, leaving the senior corporal in charge. Later that week the baby passed away, it was the worst time of my life, I had a young family to leave behind for my wife to look after, we were being bombed heavily by the Germans we were on rations and now this, what else could go possibly wrong. At the end of the week I returned and was placed in open arrest for borrowing ten shillings off another rank. This was how the officer got his own back. I was sent back to Head Quarters to await a Field General Court-Martial. Lists of names were presented to me to pick an officer to defend me. I chose one by the name of Captain Taylor. My court martial was to be held at Warley Barracks, Brentwood, Essex.

On the morning of my trial my defending officer said to me,

"Sgt, you haven't got a leg to stand on."

At the beginning of the trial I asked for the Presidents permission for me to dispense with the services of my defending officer as he had told me that I had not got much chance. This was granted to me and I pleaded guilty to the charge of borrowing money off a soldier but I had extenuating circumstances. The court listened to my story which was true and which I have related previously. I told the court of my wartime service and I was found guilty.

Chapter XX

REVERSION OF RANK

My sentence reduced me to the rank of corporal everyone was expecting me to be reverted to the rank of a private and possibly prison. I was delighted because being a corporal was the best rank in the army. This made me senior corporal in my regiment, no worry, orders which was passed down to me were passed onto the lance corporal, the only concessions I lost were being part of the Sergeants mess. I was sent to another company headquarters at Ingatestone. My first duty here was acting orderly sergeant and first parade was mounting night guard at 18.00 hours. Here was a turn up for the books, guards mounting with pick elms, some excused from wearing steel helmets, some excused from wearing boots and some excused from wearing musketry. I know the men could not help this turn out but it was a sorry do after the guards and drill that one had been used to. I started a training plan, the soldiers here had not seen *'Jerry'*, I had and he would walk over my men. So after a weekend of leave I told them to be on parade at 06.00 first light. On the first parade I noticed the smell of alcohol on the breaths of some of the men. I wasn't happy, we are at war and these troops weren't taking this seriously. We grabbed our kit and ran six miles at full pelt. Most of the men couldn't keep up. The training consisted of running every morning at 06.00, musketry on the Lee-Enfield and Tommy Gun, grenade training and compass work. It was fustrating at times some of the boys had strange jobs to do, some of them were part time working for the local farmers as Essex was a farming county. Eventually we started to be fitted out with extra kit for overseas service British North Africa Forces *BNAF* this was the only time that we were told where we were going. There was great excitement as the time drew nearer for when we would be leaving England again. I started to settle down, the hierarchy noticed not just by my standards but my men were beginning to be heads and shoulders above the rest of the battalion. I was sent for by my commanding officer and was made up to sergeant again. Most of my former sergeant pals liked this as it meant that I was junior to them now, previously I was their senior. Mind you it didn't trouble me much I was more experienced, respected by the officers and I was well up to standard in drill, fitness and weapons.

Chapter XXI

INVASION OF NORTH AFRICA

After a sea voyage of about ten days dodging enemy boats, the dreaded U-boats and Luftwaffe we arrived at Algiers, the capital of Algeria. There was much activity at this port for just previously to our landing the invasion of North Africa had started. From here we entrained for Bizerte in Tunisia the northernmost city in Africa. I say entrained but they seemed to be what we would call cattle trucks. We were to amalgamate with the 78th Infantry Division. The journey took about three days and during this time we lived a life of Nomads, so many of us piled into wagons with kit and everything. At night time as we travelled one could see behind different wagons bucket fires. These were disused old ten-gallon oil drums, holes were perforated around them and fire glowed inside just to keep us warm during the cold desert nights. When these were blazing away they would be retrieved for us by an Arab who would climb along the top of the wagon get down to the fire can and bring it back to the front of the wagon and hand it to one of us. This was an acrobatic stunt of a job which I could not have done. This he did along the train, wherever the fire buckets where. For this we did not give money but food such as biscuits, chocolate and tinned meats. Of course, we did not know that there was a food shortage in Algeria and Tunisia. We found out later that this Arab was a driver for the railway and the mate of the driver and fireman that was taking us to Bizerte. Working like this in league with one another, they weren't short of food when they got back to Algiers. I did not know that in times of peace Bizerte was a place were plenty of rich in England went on holiday but when we arrived here the port had been blasted to bits and everything was barren. Here we knew that what had happened previously in Europe just to the war starting about the enemy seizing foodstuffs and looting had also happened here. In North Africa where the enemy had been driven back by the Allies they had taken all their food with them. Most of the place was strewn with enemy tanks, roads blown up and buildings demolished. The true sense of war had been brought home to us. If this was what was happening to all conquered countries then we must fight and do our duties. Preserve our country and empire. It is worth noting that there were battalions of Palestine Jews, Arabs and Spanish, all volunteers fighting on behalf of the Allies. I got a decent job here in charge of an Italian prisoner of war camp. This is where the Italians showed me how to arm wrestle, many a time we had bets on our guys against theirs who could win at the game. They were terrible soldiers but good at football and arm wrestling. We took over from the Americans and stayed here for about six months. I will give you an instance how Jerry loved the Italians. There were two prisoner of war camps one German and one Italian. These prisoners where encamped at different parts of the town and on their way to work German and Italian prisoners would have to pass each other. As they did the German party would shout abuse and spit at the Italians. This is how two defeated allies treated each other.

* * * * * * * *

After we had completed our duties here we had our orders to go to Tunis the capital of Tunisia. This trip we did by road, all went well until we arrived just outside Tunis. Whilst the enemy had retreated he had not forgot to impede the advance of British and American forces. The Germans had mined the road quite intensely making it impossible for transport to move but also cutting off Algeria from Tunisia. Here we saw what a good job the Royal Engineers had done. They had built what we term as a Bailey bridge which is a portable pre-fabricated truss bridge made from wood and steel across rivers allowing transport to continue between the two countries We were billeted just outside Tunis itself. This city had a mixed population the largest being the Italians with a population of about forty-seven thousand. Although this was a protectorate of France during peacetime these people seemed to have held sway. The biggest trade here was on the Black Market. Blankets were being sold for ten shillings each. Here I saw men and women's two-piece suits made from these blankets. The Arabs bought stuff and sold it onto the French Tunisians, food and soap were the main shortage.

* * * * * * * *

I was chosen here to go on a mine detecting and booby trap course at a port town called Bona, now called Annaba in Algeria. The main export being rich in phosphates, lead and zinc ore which was highly valuable during a war. Vast parts of the country were mined by the Germans. After a long train journey, I arrived at my destination. The course was being run by the Royal Engineers. I found the course very interesting as well as dangerous. Both the Germans and Italians were experts at mining and boobytrapping. I will endeavour to describe here their clever ways of laying booby traps. The Italians are very artistic craftsmen and one or two cases of what they did to foil the English soldier in his advance. A soldier saw a small suitcase on the floor, the carvings on it attracted his attention so he picked it up then he proceeded to open it then suddenly there was an explosion, inside was a mine he was killed outright. Another instance when the British took over a building the commanding officer had the best room and this one room was fully furnished including a bed and a mattress. As his clerk placed some items on the bed there was a large explosion nothing was ever found of the clerk again. In laying these traps the enemy thought ahead, thinking to himself what our reactions would be in finding these attractive items. To counter this we had to denaturalize these things when we came upon them. The common items that were booby-trapped were doors, pens, taps, light switches, doorknobs and luger guns etc.

I quite enjoyed mine detecting. This operation is carried out with a mine detector and strapped to your back is a power pack. The operator advances one step at a time then sweeps the ground in front of him slightly above ground level in an arc from the nine o'clock position to the three o'clock position. If some loud shrill sounds on the detector he calls his number two who will gently prod the ground with a prodder, if a mine is detected he calls up number three who denaturalizes the device by removing the detonator. The mines are then stacked and later collected. One of the hardest mines to locate is the type that are placed in wooden boxes built up with dovetail joints. One must be very wary of these as the only metal that the detector will pick up is the metal on the tube. After passing the course I went back to my unit and was put in charge of the mine detecting squad. Our job was to clear a lane in minefields about fifteen yards wide for tanks and troops to pass through on their advance.

I was now able to get about and visit other places and to get to know their history. One of the places I visited was the Casbah in Algeria. This is the quarters that house the Arabs, a kind of city surrounded by a very high wall. Of course, this was out of bounds to troops and Europeans, but always being able to get about besides I could always buy my way around with the food and goods that people could not get. News soon gets around in a place like this I suppose that is the reason that I never got hurt or injured whist I was in the Casbah. These people like to keep their private lives and customs to themselves. I used to turn up at all odd places, once I had an invitation to a sheiks son's wedding this lasted for three days. I managed to get a seventy-two-hour pass from my unit. This part of North Africa was very hot, away from the town was even hotter because you could not get any shade just barren land. This may surprise many readers; I even came across many deserters not only British but also Germans and Italians. It made me think of the time I was on the run in Palestine, which is why I suppose I never took any action with these. The war was almost over here by now except for the cleaning up operations. With people working on the docks there did not seem much work to be done in this country, most of the daytime people were indoors because of the heat and during the night the Arabs would lie about on the footpaths and frequent the café's drinking coffee and smoking their hookah pipes. We had our orders to pack our kit and embark, our next objective was Italy.

Chapter XXII

INVASION OF ITALY

We eventually had our orders for sailing to Italy. After three days on the water we arrived at Naples, here a sad sight met our eyes. The harbour had been blown up, for disembarking it meant clambering the tops of sunken boats that had been lashed together, then planks had been placed onto these. Straight off our boat onto the next boat and we were on what was left of the quayside. Naples had a population of one million people and believe me they were destitute. I believe that since this war had started and of all the hunger struck countries that I had been too, this place was the worst. This was the country that Mussolini said that if anyone tried to invade they would be met by ten million bayonets. If this was Naples what was the other parts of Italy like! After a small amount of duty just outside of Naples we patrolled the streets having the odd skirmish and flushing out the last bit of resistance from the Italian and German troopers. On one patrol I walked into a bombed-out church and noticed a small Jesus in a crucifix position with no cross attached. I know objects could be booby trapped but this was lying on one side and I didn't see anything suspicious you could hardly see it through the rubble. I picked it up and put it in the top left pocket of my tunic it was only hand size. I carried it through the rest of the war and as soon as I arrived back in England I made a wooden cross and now is mounted on the wall at home. Another task we had to do was guard duties on the trains. I must say we were under canvas out of view but it was a good way of getting around and watching for any enemy getting aboard. We would spring on them, most of the locals would tip us off they had clearly had enough and sent to the prisoner of war camp via the Military Police.

* * * * * * * *

At meal times when the troops lined up for their meals it was terrible to see to see the small children begging them for food. Not many of our troops saw these children go without. During my stay in Italy I visited places such as Salerno, Taranto, Foggia, Florence, Rome and Milan and here one can see some fine buildings, well those still intact after the ravages of war and a land struck by famine. We heard that Mussolini the founder of Italian Fascism and dictator of Italy had been trying to escape to Switzerland with his mistress when they were apprehended in a village near Lake Como by communist partisans and subsequently executed on the 28th April 1945. On our advance through Italy no sooner than two days later after Mussolini suffering his fate news broke out amongst the ranks that Adolf Hitler had took his life in a bunker in Berlin. It was the 30th April 1945, smiles and celebrations amongst our troops. News was approaching fast, the Allies were moving towards West Berlin, the Russians on the east, the war in Italy had almost finished. Once again, we set about packing our kit and embarking though again no one knew of our destination. Once on the ship we held a sweepstake to see what part of the world we would end up.

Chapter XXIII

GIBRALTAR

Once we had finished fighting the Jerries' in Italy we moved on to Gibraltar which is a British overseas territory. It is known as the rock and had a population of about twenty-five thousand people though there were not as many from Spanish parentage as people thought. I had learned a lot about the island in my pre-war days. It was known in army terms as a home station, very isolated. During the war Gibraltar had played its part well, as there were large naval docks here. A fence divided Gibraltar and a town in Spain called La Linea, the British guarded this on the Gibraltar side. The thing that surprised me on landing here were the motorcars, no horns or claxons were heard if anyone happened to be in the way of the vehicles when approaching, continuous banging on the side of the cars or lorries would signal means of their presence by the drivers. We found out the reason, this was because the rock was the Royal Navy's radio & telegraph installation and if the proper means of letting people know of these vehicles approach they would cause interference. The Rock itself is tunnelled and inside here foodstuffs and ammunition were stored in case of a siege. These were for the garrison doing duty on the rock. I believe that the rock was about two miles round and from the base to summit is 1398 feet high. Gibraltar is a continuation of Spain but I should think that years ago there must have been a volcanic eruption which completely turned the island upside down. It is also possible that the island was once connected to North Africa, for on the rock itself are the well-known Barbary Macaques and the legend is that when the monkeys disappear so will Gibraltar.

* * * * * * * *

Our barracks were known as Buena Vista overlooking the Mediterranean Sea a nice view some will say, but not to the soldier that must do his service here. Watching ships going either way just reminded you of England, making you homesick. Our billets were made of sandstone and our beds were proper iron bedsteads. These were the only beds that we had on all our active service. These billets were bug ridden and I reckon that was why we were issued with pyjamas. Our main fatigue, which was a parade, was to strip our bedsteads every Saturday morning and treat them with special oil. This was to get rid of the bed bugs, which may be in the joints or crevasses. I believe they originated from the sandstone. The main shortage here was water, during my stay our ration was one pint of water per man per day. Most of this had to be taken over to the cookhouse for cooking and tea. This water had to be transported from Tangiers in tanks by sea. It was a strange sight that when it rained soldiers would dash out and place buckets and bowls underneath the spouts and drainpipes of their billets. This was mainly used for shaving and cleaning of teeth. Our other ablutions and washing of underclothes was done with sea water and sea water soap. The bars and cafés down in the town catered for night entertainment. Three or four Spanish girls to each café singing the same and dancing in every bar. Beer with the label on bearing the words 'John Bull,' brewed in Spain and costing one shilling and six pence about half a pint in each bottle, very expensive. You had to get a pass to visit the town. Our part here was for guard duties at the governor's palace or changing of the keys guards. This meant plenty of hard work and more spit and polish as they call it *'Bull.'* We relieved a crack peacetime regiment here, so of course we had got to bring our standards up to theirs. Most of our chaps were old timers so everyone put his shoulder to the wheel and by the time arrived for us to commence our duties we were up to the same standard. Our company commander expected the world from us but after the end of a full day training there was always moaning going on. For instance, why should our captain with just a webbing belt on for equipment keep on to us, that we should train and drill with full battle order on, oh yes, we even had officers excused from wearing equipment. The night our first guard for handing over the keys ceremony came, this was carried out each evening at 18.00hrs. I should think the whole of Gibraltar turned out this night. I was the sergeant in charge of the new guard and we passed with flying colours. The people did not expect us to turn out like this, especially just coming from service in Italy. The guard duty was for twenty-four hours on and twenty-four hours off. Most of our time was taken up in spit and polish ready for the next duty. At times we changed over with guard duties at the Generals Palace. Sometimes we could go to the Bullfights in La Linea in Spain, here on a Sunday a man can take his whole family to these affairs taking with them wine & foods for at these Bullfights they are entertained for about four hours. This was their national sport. On one of my visits here I saw a woman Bullfighter one by the name of Senorita Conchita Cintron, quite an expert too. The war was coming to an end now in Europe and it came as no surprise when the Nazis surrendered.

With our duties in Gibraltar it was also used for us to recuperate ready for the next deployment. With the news of victory in Europe most of the troops wanted to go home, but some of us wanted to set sail and help with the fight against the Japanese and finish the war. We were kept in Gibraltar as a reserve then out of the blue we heard that the Americans had dropped the atom bomb on Japan. After the atom bombs on Hiroshima and Nagasaki they too surrendered.

Chapter XXIV

HOME AND DE-MOBBED

A new government had to be elected for the coalition with Winston Churchill at its head as Prime Minister. All service personnel serving outside England could vote by proxy. The election came giving Labour a landslide. Operations were on foot now for de-mobbing. I was asked if I wanted to stay in the army but I had seen my fair share of service in peacetime and war time and it was time to leave and be with my family. I was due for release early, under the age and service group. I think I was the first to leave my company under this scheme. After an uneventful journey, by boat and train at the demobbing centre at Hereford. What a sight met our eyes, shops in billets, tailor shops and shoe shops. On reception we were waited on hand and foot. Taken for our civilian suits and shoes, fixed up with railway warrants. A kip in a nice clean bed, good sleep, good breakfast, and on the train to Birmingham and then onto Bilston. On reaching home I was surrounded by all my children and children from the neighbourhood. I decided to have a week at home before looking for work. I knew that my uphill battle had still got to continue from where it left off when I went back to the forces. I was owed six weeks holiday with pay from the forces, but I decided to get a job at Stewarts & Lloyds steelworks as a barrow filler. This firm was situated in the centre of the industrial hub of the Black Country. Here was a blast furnace which produced iron and steel. This was one of the original sites that started blast furnaces in the industrial revolution. I must state now that out of twenty-seven furnaces in the whole country my town of Bilston had eighteen of them.

Chapter XXV

BARROW FILLER

My job here was to work in a team of about twelve to keep one of the furnaces going by the way of barrow filling. Now the barrow was made of iron, the body scoop shaped, two iron handles and two big iron wheels. The barrow was filled with iron stone which we loaded out of railway trucks that when filled with the weight of stone the total weight was fifteen cubic weight. If loaded light on, that is too much on the front you could not pick the barrow off its legs. If loaded heavy on, the barrow would tip up and you would have to load again. Loaded equally you can pick up barrow and proceed to the lift which takes it to the top of the furnace, you then lowered the bell that sealed the top and emptied the contents into the furnace. I would then close the bell. At night the furnace top and surrounding area would be lit by the waste gasses burning at the *'monkey,'* a bypass pipe on top of the bell. Every third barrow is loaded with coke. A charge consisted of two loads of ironstone and one of coke. Whilst I was on this job each man did thirty-five charges. Besides these we had iron scale and turnings which one had to unload out of canal boats. This was heavy work and was run on a three-shift system.

* * * * * * * *

Eventually I was asked if I would help-out with the boating, this was because one of the boatmen was on the sick list. Being used to horses from my younger and pre-war soldiering I decided to have a bash. My mate by the name of Rhino, walked with his feet at quarter to three, but was as strong as a bullock. Each day was a different venue where we had to go to fetch our ironstone and scale, putting a load of about twenty-five tons on each canal boat. We took it in turns at the filler, which meant if we had a journey of about ten miles we would each walk ten miles on that journey. The main thing in boating is going through the locks; for instance, if you had to wait your turn at locks such as Brierley Hill which we called top of the nine, there are eight locks together so it may be a waiting time of up to two hours which would make us late finishing at the end of our day. You tie your boat outside the factory where you are going to load, the canal side nearest where your load is. You load by shovel at this stage each one of you starting at different ends of the boat, before this you will have watered and given your horse a feed of corn to be going on with. After loading so much the boat sometimes touches the bottom of the canal, *'the cut'*. You then push the boat into the centre of the canal until it gets bouncy; you then put a plank off the canal side onto the boat. This may mean a twelve-foot plank. This is where the art of filling the boat comes in. You first load your stuff in the barrow; wheel the barrow into the boat. Of course, being new to this way of boating I had to be shown. My mate said, "Harry this is the way," he started to wheel the barrow along the plank when suddenly he tumbled in and I had to go in after him and get him out, this caused a good laugh. Tunnels give one a strange experience for instance a walk of two miles through one in the Black Country, no light to guide you, all there is, is a rail at the side of the canal. You just walk behind your horse. Water keeps dripping on you off the tunnel roof, eventually to your relief you start to see daylight at the end of the tunnel. I now come to the hardest part of boating, which I believe is what boatmen call legging. You come to a tunnel where there is no towpath, you untether and un-tie your horse. Yourself and your mate lay on top of the boat back to back your feet on the roof and both together working your feet left, right, left, right pushing your boat through, this is a hard and hazardous job. On occasion your feet will catch in a part of the roof where a brick has worked loose and fallen into the water. If your boots were done up tight you could finish off with a broken ankle. That is why it was always safe to have your boots tied loosely; you must bear in mind that you cannot see the roof, as there is no light at all. In fine weather a boatman's life is not bad but winter was a testing time especially in snow when the canal was frozen and the icebreaker must clear a way for you. Fog was the biggest enemy, one day our horse was pulled in the canal, we had to get into the water to release his harness before we could get him out of the water. Many of our journeys meant me getting up at three in the morning and it was with no regrets that I got a job at a local firm as an electric furnace brass caster.

* * * * * * * *

By now our family had increased to ten children, all either going to school or under school age. This meant there was no luxury living for us as our money was taken up looking after our home and children. It was a good job that my wife knew how to cater for us, for there were a good many mouths to feed. After a period at this firm a neighbour and myself answered an advert in the local paper. It was for electric furnace brass casters. We applied and got the job though strangely enough this firm had no furnaces yet though they agreed to pay us three shillings per hour as a retainer until the furnaces were put in, as many hours as we cared to put in and extra money for Saturday and Sunday work. We just had to stand there with a sweeping brush in our hands. Eventually the furnaces arrived, when installed we started to operate them and after a given time we settled on a piece work price and you can believe me although we did our own smelting, in 1947 the wage was then £10 per week, mind you we were killing ourselves. This wage was about double to what we had been having. We were still on post-war rationing meat was limited and were only allowed nine ounces of bread a day. After a decent period at this job I could have a nine-inch television on the weekly. We were one of the first to have a television and many a time I would come back from work with the neighbours piled into to our living room watching the latest on the television.

Chapter XXVI

STREET VENDOR

As weeks went by my mate bought a small shop that came with a pony, float and a small fruit round. My friend could not drive a horse, neither could he shout out the goods that he had to sell on his round. He asked me if I wanted to buy the turnout and round for £42. This meant paying him £10 down and £2 per week. I accepted his offer. I packed in my job and visited different places that comprised this round. I went to the stable were the pony was and he took one look at me and kicked out with both his hind legs but this was no surprise as foodstuffs for animals such as corn were rationed and he was proper down the nick. I saw to it that his first meal was good followed by a helping of clover. I soon gained his affection and confidence but I did not know then that we would be partners for a decent period. I loaded up my wagon with potatoes and root vegetables ready for my first venture on the road as a street vendor. Items such as eggs, bananas, oranges and foreign apples were rationed. My first day's takings on the road were one shilling and ten pennies. I had jumped into something here as when I shouted out my wares the first question out of the mouths of the people who came to me was,

"Have you any fags."

I told them I hadn't as I made my own. Even cigarettes were rationed, if one had cigs you could get anything. What a to-do, we had won the war but everything was still rationed. I was so demoralised I could have jumped in the cut. Instead I got in touch with the local food officer and got an allocation of eggs on production of names and addresses of so called customers. I then went into Birmingham where I had an appointment with Mr Thompson who allocated me one box of bananas and one box of oranges. With these I would be able to sell my other wares as people would buy from me now I was selling such luxuries as fruit as this is what they were at the time. The wholesaler allowed me to have extra supplies from him to get more custom from me. These extras, I decided would go on my cart on Friday and Saturday as these were the days when most people had money.

Things were looking up, I was doing alright in most streets except for one, day after day I went down this street and did not sell a thing. I knew that eventually I would do some trade in this street. After about one month an old lady came out to me and said,

"Can I have six pennies of potatoes Mr, big ones for chips."

I gave her the potatoes when she tendered her sixpence I gave it back. I told her being as she had the guts to be the first in the street to buy from me she could have the potatoes with my compliments. It appeared that people did not buy from me as I was an outsider. Two other hawkers had been coming down this street all through the war and this was their domain. After this happened though I did plenty of trade down this street.

It seemed to me that I was fighting a losing battle with the local council though. They were the first in the country to start a food trades guild to call for Health & Hygiene for the goods that were being sold and for the people that handled these goods. I had to report to the food office and to the chief sanitary inspector. My orders were that my wagon had got to be covered up. This entailed me having to have the job done in aluminium at a cost of £35. I got a local wheelwright to do the job for me and allow me to pay on the weekly at £1 per week. I remember the first day on the road with my altered wagon, I was followed by two young boys. When I stopped and unlocked my covered van showing fixtures, one youngster said to the other,

"Look I told you he hadn't got any chickens in there."

The committee of the Foods Trade Guild were so pleased with my turnout that I was elected to their committee. I was the first one to be awarded a certificate for cleanness and hygiene in the whole town of Bilston. I was the only street vendor in the whole of the country to have been awarded one of these certificates. This helped me a great deal in selling my wares, for my pony was always well groomed, harness polished, brasses gleaming and his hooves always oiled and polished. My takings had gone up to about £80 per week and I was making a good profit. Keeping my wife, children and myself comfortable. By now my own class of people that used to be my fellow workers had started to boycott me for no apparent reason. As I was making steady progress they were terming me as a capitalist and therefore I was losing their custom for among my customers were a lot of middle class people. I was operating on my daily round now from eight in the morning till after six pm at night and never missed a day off the street except Sunday for four years.

* * * * * * * *

All my Sunday mornings were spent looking after my pony and cleaning down the wagon. I wasn't banking my money for I was living steady and giving my wife a decent wage. I was getting too good-natured and would listen to different people who had the knack of telling you the tale. I found that if customers could depend on me getting to their houses the same time each day they would give me their custom. I also found as time went on that plenty of women would confide in me, telling me all their troubles, they must have thought I was the family doctor! In a way I should have paid no attention because as I found out later you can become too familiar especially when it came to people paying their bills as by now I was giving people credit. I knew that the world was run on credit, but some people live on their wits which I found out as time went on. Rationing had come to an end and I was able to buy more of the fruit and luxuries that had been hard to get owing to the war. I had managed to get a fresh stable for my pony near to my home, a kind of small farm containing about a dozen cows, poultry, one horse and this character, a so-called farmer. Next to my family my pony came first in my life and all my spare time was spent looking after him and grooming him. One Saturday morning about five o'clock I went to unfasten the gates that led into the farmyard. Outside were two men, I knew who they were, the weights and inspector's men. They had found out that another vendor had been watering the milk down and they had tested the previous evenings milking that was already in cans waiting to be collected. These cans were not collected that morning as he was tried at court and had to pay a big fine. Someone jealous of my trade must have told them I was doing the same so they turned up uninvited hoping to catch me out. I was doing my best to play the game by giving fair weight and giving proper service but when I looked back I may have done better if I had been craftier and had been not so straightforward with my customers.

Chapter XXVII

SHOP AND MOBILE COACH

One day I met one of the town councillors who said to me "Harry have you put your name down for one of the new shops that they are putting up at the other end of town." I said no and told him he was a *Tory*. I had not seen any new shops being built. What chance had I got? I had my family with ten children and I was only a street vendor. "Put your name down," he said, "the council think highly of you as you carried out their instructions on their bylaws." I contacted my old friend Ben Bilboe and he confirmed this was the case. Out of all the applications that were sent into the council I was picked out and asked if I would accept the tenancy of a greengrocers and wet fish shop that was being erected. I jumped at the chance; this was in April but I had to wait for the shop to be completed before I could move in which was eight months later in December. The Stowlawn estate was built on the land which is situated between Stowheath and the Villiers. The area was a mix of wasteland and old mining shafts with a rusty brook and a pink pool. The area was flattened, dips and bumps filled in with hardcore from bombed out buildings in London. The council wanted something new and unusual for a post war housing estate so they employed the help of an architect by the name of Otto Neurath, a Viennese Philosopher, who later passed away, so a lady by the name of Ella Briggs became the main architect. Shocked by the poverty and poor housing within the area they designed and built an estate. Using the labour of some German Prisoners of War they painted the houses white surrounding them by greens, shops, a school and a public house, we couldn't wait to move in.

* * * * * * * *

There was only one thing that marred our jubilation, one of my daughters 'Jean' was stricken down by a stroke that left her dumb, blind and paralysed. I used to sit with her for about four hours every day as she lay in hospital. She eventually died eight days later from a combination of Tuberculosis and Meningitis having been in a coma for some time. It took a great deal of time for us to get over this for to lose a child who was just fifteen years of age was a big blow.

One day my old friend Ben Bilboe said to me, "There are only two things that I am waiting for and that is to see the day come for you to open your shop and for me to give you an invitation to visit the Houses of Parliament." He had been elected as a prospective candidate for the Ormskirk division of Lancashire. Three days after telling me this he died. Gone was my old pal of our fighting days, a bitter blow to the town that he had represented for the past seventeen years, it was September 1951.

* * * * * * * *

We moved into the new shop in December without any capital at all. The money that I had was spent on purchasing scales, fittings, etc. My shop was stocked on goods which I had obtained on credit. Thinking the shop would pay its way on this big post war council housing estate of Stowlawn. I even sold my pony & wagon. This is where I made a big mistake as I found out it was easier for me to take goods to a person's door because if a person wanted to come to the shop they must first get cleaned and tided up, wearing their best clobber and bring their children with them. After about one month I decided to trade on the streets again. Having sold my turnout there was no alternative but to get myself a van. This I obtained on credit and with the help of a pal who gave me driving lessons and came with me around the streets, eventually I could start up a new round. I can say now though that I drove for three years without taking a driving test. I found that when my trade picked up on my round that business improved in my shop which meant that my wife and daughters had to work in the shop. While I was doing well with the shop and the mobile coach I had the opportunity to purchase a few cars over the years. I bought an Austin 16, it was, as you would say nowadays a 2.2 litre. The number 16 being the calculation determined by the road tax office to how much road tax you paid. It had a built in hydraulic jacking system operated from a pump located under the bonnet with a top speed of 75mph. Another car I purchased was an Austin Sheerline, it was a luxurious car at the time competing with that of a Rolls Royce or a Bentley. It was a very heavy car weighing nearly two ton and a top speed of 82mph.

* * * * * * * *

After a dispute with the other shopkeepers over selling each other's goods the council gave us permission to sell what goods would bring us the biggest profit. This was a free for all; I got myself a coach and converted it into a mobile shop. I now had to employ one of my son in laws to help me on my rounds. Business boomed and by now we were selling everything such as greengrocery, grocery, haberdashery, frozen foods, sweets confectionary, baby foods, cakes, and tobacco. With all these goods some of them became a luxury for people that were using credit and some of their weekly bills were huge.

This is where you could say some were living on their wits. I should have taken a firm stand for when the time came as they could not pay their bills, they would use all the excuses known to man. One day one of my customers came to see me and said he couldn't pay his tab but he had a monkey that I could have for payment. I thought it would be a good idea and better than not getting any money at all. So, I said, "yes, I'll have it," and the next day during my round on the mobile shop he brought it out and I took it back to the shop. I got to be quite fond of it until one day he escaped and got onto the roof of the houses at the back of the shop. It started ripping the tiles from the roofs and then disappeared down Mrs Browns chimney staying there for three days ransacking through people's houses. I got Fred Wolverson, who later became the Mayor of Bilston to climb on the roof and the monkey jumped off landing in my arms with his head sticking out of a chimney pot. On another occasion I brought back an Orangutan in a cage, on the back of the van. The wife went mad and said, "it's either him or me, we have enough bloody kids." So, I took it to Coles of Bilston a well-known business that was owned by William Cole, which he had since the 1920's specialising in goods reclaimed from household demolitions. As the business grew he built a private zoo to help attract customers. It was on the Great Bridge Road in Bilston. He had a lion, a few bears and even some monkeys and now he had my orangutan. He was happy to have him and it made the Express & Star newspaper that weekend.

When the time came for customers to pay their bill, they would say that the husband had been on the panel, have had to pay the electric bill or make up the arrears of rent and other excuses. Some were even saying to their neighbours, "Oh Harry is not bad, tell him you can't pay, he won't say anything." Never a week went by without someone telling me they could not pay. This was getting me nowhere for I could see the profit that I should have been getting from my business was not going to be. If a customer could not pay me I lost their money, profit I should have had from it and their future custom, so you see I was hit three ways. People got into the habit of borrowing their rent arrears off me or asking me to pay their electric bills for them. Most of this money I never saw again. Therefore, if I was getting no money for half my goods how was I to carry on. I once loaned a fellow £50 after he had an accident and he was going to pay me back out of his compensation. Three days before he was due to pick up his money he died so you see how fate was treating me. My takings by now were in the region of £550 for both the shop and mobile coach, but owing to bad payers and other things, I myself could not pay my way. When it came my turn to pay my creditors I had to resort to robbing Peter to pay Paul. If at any time I could not pay one of my creditors I had to take the money that I had put on one side to pay another creditor to give him and so on. Things went on like this for a time, until at last the Sheriffs Officer was forced to call on me for money that I should have sent to firms. The one that called often at my place had no difficulty at all in extracting money from me. He didn't care how he got the money as long as he got it because he got to keep a percentage of it. Of course, if you couldn't pay there was no alternative but prison. I could not carry on any longer so my biggest creditor said that if I let him have my business he would pay my creditors, what choice did I have. I then had an offer to become manager of a public house and seeing that it would be a shelter for my family I accepted it.

Chapter XXVIII

MANAGER

Coming out of the shop the council was under no obligation to find me a house. Before taking over the public house I had an agreement drawn up at the accountants. The fellow that had my business called at each creditor and asked if he settled my account with them, would they accept five shillings in the pound. This they agreed upon. So now to all intents and purposes my troubles were over. The inn that I had taken over was fifty yards from the local police station called the Globe Inn on Mount Pleasant, Bilston. It was opposite the Theatre Royal and next door was the police station, it was known locally as the *'Gluepot'* and it was of ill repute situated. It was the haunt of pimps, prostitutes, thieves and the odd London gangster. After a while I went to the station and asked them if they knew what sort of place I was keeping, "yes," they said, "but if they do no wrong at your place you are in the clear, besides when we want to pick them up we know where they will be." We had a renowned London gangster come in with his heavies by the name of Jack *'The Spot'* Comer while he was in the area looking to setting up illegal betting shops. Randolph Turpin, a champion boxer came in once he was from Leamington Spa. Also, another boxer, Johnny Prescott who won his first fight in Wolverhampton used to frequent the Inn, he went on to win the British and Commonwealth titles. He fought Henry Cooper at Birmingham City football ground. In 1970 he was out pointed by Joe Bugner and called it a day.

After three months of me being at the inn my telephone was forever ringing. The calls were from my former creditors asking me to be a gentleman and pay my debts. I could not stand this any longer so I rang my former accountant to tell him what had happened. I read the agreement over the phone to him. "Oh, that," he said, "that is not worth the paper it is written on." When I came to have a good look at it he was right. He had not put a date on or signed it. Yes, I had been taken for a ride alright. There was nothing I could do about it I just had to pay the best way I could, so with the help of my family I managed to pay to the best of my ability.

In the meantime, life in this pub was not as one would like it to be, the worst reputation in the town. Fights between whites and blacks were very frequent; I have taken guns, bayonets and razors off customers.

On one occasion a Cuban with a body guard of six Maltese came to sort out a white man and a woman. One had a gun so someone fetched the Police. When they came into the smoke room, the woman said, "one of them as got a gun." The police asked, "Is that right Harry." I had to think quickly, "No," I said, "If they leave now I prefer no charges," they left; it was possible that if I had said yes someone would have got shot. These same men came back one night to thank me. I got to know all the news that was going on in the area. The work of all the prostitutes and pimps, in fact all the distasteful things in life. I can honestly say that for all the notorious people that came into this pub I never accepted a drink off them, not even a cigarette for I know what the consequences would have been. One chap who spent most of his time in the place, once had a bottle of beer bought for him, he received eighteen months in prison for living on the immoral earnings of a prostitute. Mind you he was always in their company.

* * * * * * * *

Wherever you find women men will follow, so even if you sold tea in these sorts of places you would still sell plenty. I still had to keep my eyes open; I knew the comings and goings of all who came into my place. Yes, even businessmen made periodic visits. After two years of this life and still paying my creditors, it was no wonder I was reported missing through loss of memory. I don't know what happened to me until my sons and son in laws picked me up at Paddington, London. I believe I had been in hospital in St Mary's Paddington. When my doctor visited me, I had to be confined to bed for a few days and he told me the best thing that I could do was to file my petition for bankruptcy. The pub was finally demolished in the 1960's.

Chapter XXIX

BANKRUPT

Before I talk of a person going bankrupt I must tell you that at different times I stood bail on behalf of characters that had been sentenced for trial at Stafford Assizes. I also spoke in their defence, one was a hardened criminal who was expecting seven years PD (Previous Detention) it happened to be my nephew Walter Groom and he only got three years, but still managed to escape from Dana Prison more commonly known as Shrewsbury Prison the only person to do so.

First week in February I went to the County Court to tell them I would file my petition for bankruptcy. "This will cost you ten pounds," they said, I was astounded, "ten pounds," I said, "I haven't got a penny, if I have got nothing how can I find ten pounds." "That is the law," I was told. I came back home and one of my sons gave me the money. I paid this but only got a receipt for five pounds when I asked the reason for this I was told the receipt was for my application to go bankrupt the other five pounds was to the official receiver to help in the cost of office staff. I do remember a judge who asked a person once why he had not gone bankrupt sooner and when the man said he did not know that one had to pay this money before he could file his petition. I am trying to put everyone in the picture of what happens once you have filed your petition. This I must say, once you have completed your form at the County Court you are told to wait for a fellow from the official receivers to come and ask you questions. I waited and when he came he took me home and asked me questions. While I was at the County Court he had already been to my house to mark goods etc, and told my wife not to touch anything. If this was not done you could go home and remove what you wanted while you were waiting for him to call at your home. This must be done or else people would be going bankrupt all the time. He seized all documents, life insurance, and bills, receipts etc. He asked if my wife had property, bank accounts, cars, fur coats, jewellery, etc any money hoarded away. The thing that you value the most is a blue paper, stating that you have filed your petition for bankruptcy. If anyone calls on you for debts you just show this paper and they should leave you alone and not harass you for monies owed. I was glad to get this, for believe me some of my creditors had given me a dog's life in the last three to four years. When I could not pay they had threatened me with prison, yes, the lot. It seemed a kind of blackmail to some of them for they thought by threatening me they could get me to pay. It also states on this paper that if you have credit to over ten pounds without disclosing that you are bankrupt you are liable to prison. If I had been a dishonest person I could have transferred my business to my wife and then I should have been all right, but no I wanted to be genuine and then my conscience would be clear.

* * * * * * * *

I had to report to Birmingham each day for a week. An examiner questioned, me starting with my name, date of birth, history right through your life then they compile everything you tell them, cross examining you to try to catch you out. If your mind is clear your answers are correct as were in my case therefore I had nothing to hide. My examiner had plenty to write. I bet he was glad when it was all over, the same as me. My biggest snag was that three years previously my accountant had shown me to have nearly four thousand pounds to my credit. We had a big argument over this and at the finish I was accused of having shared this with my biggest creditor, the same fellow that had my business. Things were going bad for me so I asked the examiner to get my accountant on the phone. This he did and he again said that I had this sum to my credit. I said ask him if he ever saw this money, he did and he said he had never seen it. I told him he was the same fellow that had made out the agreement that he now had, yes, the same one that contained no date or signature. After you have been through all this your name appears in the local paper under the heading of the London Gazette. It was three days after my name appeared that my old friend from the sheriffs' office appeared once more, this time he got his answer in a no uncertain manner. The last thing that you do at the official receivers is to state the exact sums that you owe your creditors, you are then given the blue paper declaring that you are bankrupt, if any creditors press you for money, you just show them this and they won't bother you anymore. At the same time, you yourself cannot obtain credit. All my goods at the public house were taken from me except for six beds, they left me with these. One thing was that the van that collects your goods has no name on it so people are none the wiser.

Chapter XXX

HOUSE HUNTING

My next problem was to get out of the pub and find somewhere to live. There were no houses available at the local council so of course I would have to wait my turn on the housing list. I had to get accommodation for fourteen of us as the licensing law states that anyone who is bankrupt cannot hold a license to sell ale or to keep a public house. I must be fair to the local council officers for the kindness they showed to me. I was able to see the town clerk and housing manager without fixing up an appointment. They told me that if there was a house for sale they would buy it and mortgage it in one of my son in laws names. Unfortunately, I had no such luck in finding one.

One day going around my usual jaunts looking for a house I came to a house that the council had bought under the compulsory house purchase scheme. It was empty, windows smashed in, electric fittings gone, fireplaces, lead piping missing, outside toilet smashed up, it only wanted the bulldozer to finish it off as the tatters and vandals had done the rest. I saw the housing manager, he said it would take too much of the rate payers money to have the repairs carried out, but if I could do anything then certainly I would be able move in. I dreaded showing my wife and when I did she cried, saying "to think we have come to this." A friend of mine was demolishing a property opposite this house he gave me doors and window frames and fireplaces, toilet and sink. My sons and son in laws set about the transformation of this house which contained four bedrooms, and three rooms downstairs. I must state also that the electric board allowed my wife £10 credit by wiring and fixing new electric lights. I was not allowed by law to ask for credit. Three months had gone by since I had filed my petition, we moved into the house in Frost Street Ettingshall, Bilston. There was no rent to pay for the first month, then only nineteen shillings per week. I still cannot thank my local council enough for no one could be more humane than these. In the three years we lived there they re-housed six of my family.

Chapter XXXI

GETTING A JOB

We left the public house with no misgivings, glad to get out of it. I had three days straightening up in the house and got myself a job at the foundry opposite. It was 1964, I was fifty-six years of age and after doing no manual work for the past sixteen years I took a job on a cupola, to melt the iron for the moulders to cast. I could put in as many hours as I wanted but this foundry left a lot to be desired. There were no proper toilets, it was out of date. I would get out of this as soon as I got a chance to change my job. I got that chance when I had got to go on short time. I applied for a job at my previous employers Joseph Sankey & Sons in Albert Street, Bilston. I explained my case, told them everything and they gave me the job of labourer and degreaser. People often asked me if I was happy doing my work, when I told them yes, they thought I was mad. Although I am a shop-steward and although I do what I can for my members I also think of the management who gave me employment at the most critical time of my life. I get on with my fellow workers and it seems funny how they come to me for advice not only on work but also domestic issues. There are fine unions in operation at the factory, there has been one or two little upsets, nothing to shout about. I find that talking around the table with management, talking in their language many a difficulty can be solved in this way. I believe everybody can be happy. After years of battling what seemed to be me against the world I have concluded that things are not too bad, not for us in Britain at any rate.

In 1966 we finally moved for the last time to Lawley Road Bilston, a close-knit neighbourhood. I knew most families in the area, this was either by having the shop or pub. I also knew people from working at Stewart & Lloyds steel works which was later taken over by British Steel and still employed many people from the area. Many a Sunday night was taken up at the social club. The Steel Works eventually closed in April 1980 a loss to the area economically.

There was a new war that they were calling the cold war and with it came the threat of wiping one another off the planet. The atom bombs which fell on Japan in the Second World War were small compared to today's nuclear bombs. Thirty-five years after the end of the Second World War technology was advancing, even landing man on the moon. I have always had a good memory for remembering places, people and dates. I am gifted on most subjects and sports. The 1960's looked promising we were doing well as a nation and the economy was doing well, British business on the up. None of the youngsters needed to struggle through wars or in between wars like I did. They had new music to listen to which sounded completely different to when I was growing up.

Out of the countries I have visited and the different people I have had the pleasure of living with, in peace as well as in war, I have no hesitation in stating that Great Britain is by far the best. For one thing you get freedom of speech and the most treasured is that you are innocent by law until proven guilty. I have my own reasons and beliefs of how different things tend to appear to me in this world. People often say to me, 'would you go through all this again' and yes, I would, for although my life has been rough and tough the life and adventure cost me nothing but it cost the government thousands of pounds.

In the early part of my life I was a good Christian. It was taught in school through Religious Education then somehow, I developed an agnostic attitude to religious beliefs, questioning everything. Seeing war, starvation and hardship at the uppermost level led me asking, "well if there is a god why are we doing this, or why is a god letting this happen?"

In my retirement I write poetry and have published a few poems. I still try to be active in the community. I have many a visit from the local Members of Parliament, the local Labour MP Robert Edwards and Enoch Powell the Conservative MP. I am also good pals with the local Mayor Walter Hughes who also writes science fiction books.

I have sent a letter and poems to HRH The Duke & Duchess of Windsor and received acknowledgment and thanks. I have sent the Prime Minister a letter and three poems relating to the country, this was also acknowledged with thanks from Downing Street. A letter and poem to Her Majesty Queen Elizabeth on her state visit to West Germany, in 1970 this also was acknowledged with thanks from Buckingham Palace and a letter from President Johnson of the United States of America. Also, a signed letter from the Pope.

I sometimes get asked to give lectures to students and I enjoy writing articles for our local history newspaper the Black Country Bugle and have appeared on a couple of BBC documentaries about the Black Country. I also wrote a manuscript on 'Battery Operated Vehicles from 1837-1969.' Who would have thought fifty years on the car manufacturers would still be trying to develop a car to run solely on battery power?

Well that's my story and I'm sure there are many stories like it.

Thank you for reading 'Harry'

H Southall-Owen 28th January 1908-23rd January 2000

Printed in Great Britain
by Amazon